Elvis

American Idol

Susan Doll, Ph.D.

Publications International, Ltd.

Susan Doll holds a Ph.D. in radio, television, and film studies from Northwestern University and is an instructor of film studies at Oakton Community College, Des Plaines, Illinois. She also writes articles and reviews on film, pop culture, and history for various journals and magazines. In addition, Susan works for Facets Multi-Media as a writer and researcher. She is the author of *Elvis: A Tribute to His Life, The Films of Elvis Presley, Elvis for Dummies, Best of Elvis, Marilyn: Her Life and Legend, Understanding Elvis, Elvis—Forever in the Groove,* and *On Location Florida: Filmmaking in the Sunshine State.*

Page 124: Excerpt from *Films in Review,* by Henry Hart. Copyright © December 1965. Used with permission from Roy Frumkes, editor *Films in Review.*

Page 165: © 2005 Andy Warhol Foundation for the Visual Arts/ARS, New York.

Louis Weber, CEO
Publications International, Ltd.
7373 North Cicero Avenue
Lincolnwood, Illinois 60712

Manufactured in China.

8 7 6 5 4 3 2 1

ISBN-13: 978-1-4127-1249-1
ISBN-10: 1-4127-1249-1

Library of Congress Control Number: 2010926734

Contents

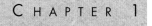

Follow That Dream:

From Tupelo to Memphis

"Before Elvis, there was nothing."

—John Lennon

*Elvis, age 2, with his parents,
Gladys and Vernon*

ELVIS ARON PRESLEY was born to Vernon and Gladys Love Presley on January 8, 1935, in East Tupelo, Mississippi. Like many residents of East Tupelo, the Presleys were poor. They lived in a two-room shotgun shack (right) that Vernon had built the previous year. The family moved several times when Elvis was a child, and Vernon worked at a number of jobs to support his wife and child. Despite many hardships, the Presleys were close to their extended family in the Tupelo area, and they enjoyed belonging to the First Assembly of God Church. In September 1948, they moved to Memphis because the city promised better job opportunities.

Elvis learned how to play the guitar in Tupelo and showed an early interest in music. In Memphis, he was exposed to gospel, rhythm-and-blues, and country music, which he would later integrate to form his unique sound. Music became the path that would lead Elvis and his family to a better life.

Elvis Presley "is a mystery that may never be solved."

—Journalist Nick Tosches

"I don't regard money or position as important. But I can never forget the longing to be someone. I guess *if you are poor,* you always *think bigger and want more* than those who have everything when they are born."

—*Elvis Presley, Time, May 7, 1965*

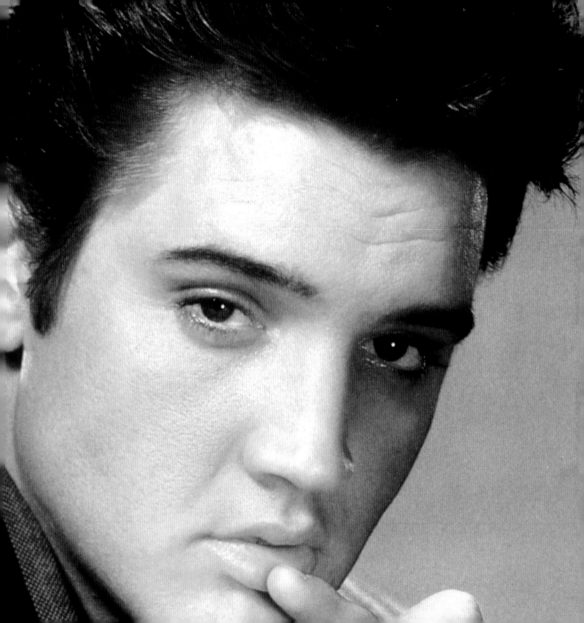

Elvis: Scandinavian and/or Anglo-Saxon for **"all wise, sage."** The name is probably a derivative of Alvis, which is Old Norse for "all wise." In Norse mythology, Alvis was the name of a dwarf who was set to marry Thor's daughter, Thrud. Thor tricked Alvis by asking him questions until the sun rose, at which time the dwarf turned into stone.

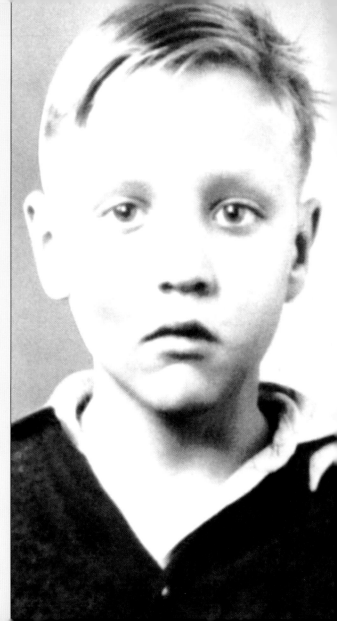

Gladys Presley

Gladys Love Smith was born in Pontonoc County, Mississippi, which, compared to Tupelo, was deep in the backwoods. Born into a large family, Gladys shared what little the family had with seven brothers and sisters. Her father, who was a sharecropper and possibly a moonshiner, died when Gladys was a teenager. She was forced to work to help support her family because her mother was frail and sick. When she was 21, she met handsome Vernon Presley, who was 17 years old. After a whirlwind two-month courtship, the couple married, but they lied about their

Gladys and Elvis Presley

ages on the marriage license. She said she was 19, and he claimed to be 21. When she became pregnant, she was certain she was going to have twins, though few believed her. Sadly, one of the twins, Jessie Garon, was stillborn.

Gladys was once a tall, thin, attractive woman, with dark hair and eyes. Throughout much of her life, she seemed plagued by a kind of melancholy, perhaps the result of so much misfortune at such a young age. However, Gladys will always be remembered for the depth of her love for her surviving son, Elvis Aron.

JUST the Facts

Tupelo

- Tupelo was founded in 1859 and incorporated in 1870.

- Tupelo is named after the tupelo tree (also known as black gum tree).

- Tupelo National Battlefield is the site of the Battle of Tupelo, the last major battle fought in Mississippi during the Civil War.

- One of the deadliest tornadoes in history swept through Tupelo on April 5, 1936, killing 216 people.

- Tupelo is located along the Natchez Trace, a road that is older than America itself.

- In 1933, Tupelo became the first city to purchase power from the Tennessee Valley Authority (the TVA).

Myth vs. Fact

Legend has it that Elvis entered the talent contest at the *Mississippi–Alabama Fair and Dairy Show* in 1945 and won second place for singing "Old Shep." Made famous by Red Foley, the song is a ballad about a boy and his dearly departed dog. Elvis's prize supposedly consisted of free passes for the fair rides, plus five dollars. In very early versions of this story, Elvis was even said to have won the contest.

Research done by Bill Burk for his book *Early Elvis: The Tupelo Years* has dispelled this myth. A bespectacled Elvis did sing "Old Shep," but interviews with Tupelo residents and this old, crinkled photo of the contestants (right) reveal that the young boy did not win anything. At best, he may have placed fifth.

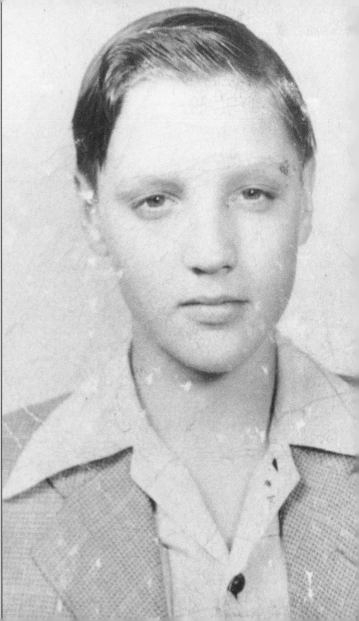

"My daddy knew a lot of *guitar players,* and most of them **didn't work,** so he said, 'You should make up your mind to either be a guitar player or an electrician, but I never saw a guitar player that was worth a damn.'"

—*Elvis, from the documentary* Elvis on Tour, 1972

Even in elementary school, *Elvis* was attracted to girls and vice versa. His last *"romance"* before moving to Memphis was with Magdalene Morgan, who attended Lawhon Elementary School and the First Assembly of God Church with Elvis.

Mississippi Slim

Elvis learned about traditional country music from Mississippi Slim, whose real name was Carvel Lee Ausborn. Slim was a native of Tupelo and a fixture on local radio station WELO for more than 20 years. Elvis, who was friends with Slim's younger brother James, may have learned several guitar chords from Slim. Elvis's uncle Vester Presley also taught the young boy how to handle and play a guitar. It's possible that Elvis sang on WELO's amateur radio show called "Black and White Jamboree" (also known as "Saturday Jamboree"). Named for the Black and White hardware store, the Saturday afternoon program featured a live studio audience. Locals were allowed to perform on the program on a first-come, first-served basis. Elvis attended the show regularly, and he may have sung the traditional ballad "Old Shep" on the air when he was eight or nine.

In August 1956, after a visit to his barber, Elvis clowned around with one of Memphis's finest.

We figured if we went to Memphis there would be **more money** and it would be **more fun** for Elvis, but in the early days we were bitterly disappointed. His mother and I walked the streets looking for work. We did this even in heavy rain or snow but for quite some time, there was no work to be found."

—*Vernon Presley*

Elvis Lived Where?

370 Washington Street—the first Memphis address for the Presleys

572 Poplar Avenue

185 Winchester Street, Apartment 328—in a housing project called *Lauderdale Courts*

The Presleys lived in Lauderdale Courts from September 1949 to January 1953.

698 Saffarans Street

462 Alabama Street—Elvis lived here when he first recorded at Sun Studio

2414 Lamar Avenue

1034 Audubon Drive—the first house Elvis bought after becoming a professional singer

3764 Elvis Presley Boulevard—*Graceland*

Vernon and Gladys pose proudly alongside their son's growing fleet of cars at their home on Audubon Drive.

For Elvis, Graceland was much more than just a place to live: It was the one place where he could be himself without a media frenzy.

Elvis and his friends often went to the movies, and their favorite films were westerns. Here, *Elvis* displays his *quick draw.*

Elvis hangs out with his ***closest friends,*** who also lived in Lauderdale Courts. From left: Farley Guy, Elvis, Paul Dougher, and Buzzy Forbess.

L. C. Humes High School

- Elvis attended Humes High from 1949 to 1953.

- The school was named after Laurence Carl Humes, a former president of the Memphis Board of Education.

- In 1952, Elvis attempted to join the school's football team, the Tigers.

- The school's yearbook was called the *Herald*.

- On April 9, 1953, Elvis appeared in the school's annual Minstrel Show, though the program misspelled his name as "Elvis Prestly."

- The school is currently a junior high called Humes Middle School.

One of Elvis's classes at Humes High

Poplar Tunes, founded by hardworking Joe Cuoghi, epitomizes the 1950s record shop. Located near Lauderdale Courts, the one-story brick building was a hangout for Elvis and his friends during their high school years. As a youth, Elvis purchased singles at Poplar Tunes to add to his ever-growing record collection. When he went from being a record collector to a recording artist, Poplar Tunes began selling his Sun singles. Most claim it was the first store to sell an Elvis Presley record. Because Elvis was from the neighborhood, his singles sold like wildfire, and he enjoyed signing autographs at the store for the local customers who supported him. Poplar Tunes still sells Elvis's records, and it looks much the same as it did in 1954. The walls of the store

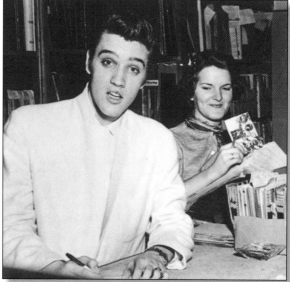

Elvis at Poplar Tunes

are lined with dozens of rare and interesting photos, including a telling shot of Elvis, Dewey Phillips, and Cuoghi that captures that fleeting moment when Elvis—standing between obscurity and legend—was just a boy from the neighborhood who made good.

ELVIS'S EARLY FAVORITES

GOSPEL MUSIC

Local gospel groups at Ellis Auditorium

Blackwood Brothers Quartet

Hovie Lister and the Statesman,
especially lead singer Jake Hess

BLUES MUSIC

Local performers at Green Owl
on Beale Street

Lowell Fulson at Club Handy
on Beale Street

Dewey Phillips's "Red Hot and Blue"
show on WHBQ

Arthur "Big Boy" Crudup

Arthur Gunter

COUNTRY MUSIC

Eddy Arnold

Louvin Brothers (Gladys Presley's favorite)

Grand Ole Opry

Bob Neal's "High Noon Round-Up" show
on WMPS

*Even as a teenager, Elvis had an impressive
record collection.*

POP MUSIC

Dean Martin

Mario Lanza

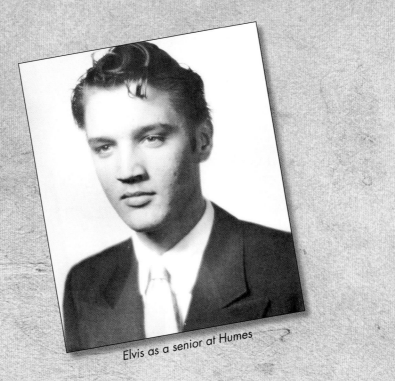

Elvis as a senior at Humes

"We talked about *getting jobs* when we got out of Humes; of *making a decent living.* Elvis always said he wanted a job where he could provide for his mother and father."

—*Buzzy Forbess,* **Early Elvis: The Humes Years**

Elvis's EARLY RÉSUMÉ

1950 Mowing lawns

    Loew's State Theater

1951 Precision Tool

    Loew's State Theater

1952 MARL Metal Products

1953 M.B. Parker Machinists

    Precision Tool

1954 Crown Electric

Loew's State Theater

At the Movies

According to accounts from his high-school friends, Elvis enjoyed going to the movies. The movies he saw included:

Tarzan

The *Tarzan* series, starring Johnny Weissmuller

City Across the River (1949), starring Tony Curtis, Stephen McNally, and Thelma Ritter

Samson and Delilah (1949), starring Victor Mature, Hedy Lamarr, and Angela Lansbury

Son of Ali Baba (1952), starring Tony Curtis and Piper Laurie

Houdini (1953), starring Tony Curtis and Janet Leigh

The Great Diamond Robbery (1953), starring Red Skelton - - - - - - - - - - - - - - - - - - -

The Blackboard Jungle (1955), starring Glenn Ford, Vic Morrow, and Sidney Poitier

East of Eden (1955), starring James Dean, Julie Harris, Jo Van Fleet, and Raymond Massey

Rebel Without a Cause

(1955), starring James Dean, Natalie Wood, and Sal Mineo - - - - - - - - -

Elvis was watching **The Great Diamond Robbery** when Dewey Phillips called him to WHBQ for his first radio interview.

Rebel Without a Cause

WDIA

WDIA radio went on the air for the first time in 1947 with a rotation of classical, pop, and country music. Each program was between 15 and 60 minutes, and the station broadcast only during the day. However, the station's owners, Bert Ferguson and John R. Pepper III, had always entertained the idea of reaching out to Memphis's African American community, which constituted 40 percent of the city's population. In 1948, they hired Nat D. Williams, a former teacher and journalist, to host "Brown America Speaks," a program featuring prominent black spokespersons and personalities. By October, WDIA was broadcasting music segments and other programs directed at Memphis's black population, earning the nickname "the Mother Station of the Negroes." Local blues artist B. B. King hosted a musical segment and sometimes played his own music as well as that of other local rhythm-and-blues performers. Other programs featured gospel music.

The influence of blues and rhythm-and-blues on Elvis's music cannot be underestimated, and a source for that music was WDIA. The station is often remembered for its connection to Elvis's musical style. However, at the time, the station was far more important for the services it provided for the black community. WDIA hosted musical events called "Goodwill Revues," and some of the ticket sales went to such charitable projects as the Goodfellows Christmas Basket Fund, summer baseball teams, and transportation for handicapped black children to get to school.

B. B. King

Lansky's on Beale Street

- Lansky Bros. Men's Shop, whose clientele included local blues and rhythm-and-blues artists, was Elvis's favorite place to buy clothes.

- Lansky's was located at 126 Beale Street in Memphis.

- Elvis began shopping there in 1952.

- When Elvis died in 1977, Lansky's provided suits for the pallbearers.

- Lansky's closed in 1980.

- Elvis's preference for colorful, hip, and sometimes loud attire became his signature style, along with turned-up collars and skinny belts with the buckle to the side.

CHAPTER 2

All Shook Up:
Rock 'n' Roll Rebel

"Despite repeated efforts by critics to cool his sex-hot flame, Elvis Presley has remained *the most incendiary figure* in the world of rock 'n' roll."

—Newsweek, *August 27, 1956*

A LOOK BACK AT THE BEGINNING of Elvis Presley's career offers a glimpse at a fascinating time in music history and an important era in American society. Elvis combined a variety of musical genres—blues, country, rhythm-and-blues—that exploded into an entirely new sound when they came pouring from his soul. Eventually dubbed "rockabilly," his music became one of the core sounds of rock 'n' roll. Not only was his music influential but his performing style, clothing choice, and hairstyle helped define a young generation eager to disassociate itself from past fashions and tastes. Not to be forgotten is the state of the pop music industry at the time, which was flexible enough to allow tiny record companies and regional radio stations to break new sounds with new artists.

Myth vs. Fact

On a Saturday afternoon late in the summer of 1953, 18-year-old Elvis Presley entered the **Memphis Recording Service.** Rock 'n' roll folklore holds that a naive young Elvis went to the studio that day to make a record for his mother's birthday. As late as 1968, an article by respected music critic Robert Hilburn repeated this apocryphal story. However, because Gladys Presley's birthday was April 25, the timing in this version of events does not add up. While no one knows for sure what prompted Elvis to go to the studio that day, one likely explanation paints him as being more ambitious than the Elvis folklore suggests. More than likely, Gladys's birthday was the last thing on his mind, because Elvis was looking to get discovered. He recorded "My Happiness" (originally by the Ink Spots) for his acetate, backed by "That's When Your Heartaches Begin."

RECORDS THAT SELL!

SUN RECORD COMPANY
INCORPORATED

639 MADISON   MEMPHIS, TENN.

TO:

POSTMASTER: CONTENTS: MERCHANDISE. MAY BE OPENED FOR INSPECTION

Sun Studio/Memphis Recording Service

"I'll Never Stand in Your Way"

Elvis recorded this song in January 1954 on his second trip to the Memphis Recording Service. He hoped to attract the attention of Sam Phillips. On the back of this acetate is his version of "It Wouldn't Be the Same Without You."

"I'll Never Stand in Your Way," written by Fred Rose and Hy Heath, was well known at the time Elvis strolled through the door to make his second acetate. Joni James had enjoyed modest success with it in November 1953, and a few days after her record hit the stores, Ernie Lee released his version. "It Wouldn't Be the Same Without You" was recorded by country singer Jimmy Wakely during the 1940s.

Sam Phillips

Born in 1923 and raised just outside of Florence, Alabama, Sam Cornelius Phillips was greatly influenced by his rural Southern roots. Working in the cotton fields, Phillips was exposed to gospel and blues music, and he experienced the poverty and hard life of many Depression-era families. As a record producer, he drew on those experiences to shape a new musical aesthetic—a purely Southern sound that combined rhythm-and-blues and country-western with a hardscrabble philosophy born of bad times. The music that emerged—a Dixie-fried sound

Sam Phillips with Elvis

called rockabilly—would emanate from Phillips's Sun Records in the mid–1950s and influence all of rock 'n' roll.

Phillips's genius lay in recognizing the talented singers and musicians of the region. Of his desire to record Southern-based music, Phillips reportedly mused, "I just knew this was culture, and it was so embedded in these people because of hardship . . . Generation after generation, these people have been overlooked—black and white!" For his contribution in shaping modern music, Phillips was inducted into the Rock and Roll Hall of Fame in 1986.

Marion Keisker

Most Elvis fans know that Marion Keisker was working as a receptionist at Sun Studio the day Elvis recorded his first acetate, but few know of Keisker's other accomplishments.

- Before working for the Memphis Recording Service/Sun Studio, Keisker was a Memphis radio personality on WREC, hosting a talk show called "Meet Kitty Kelly" among other programs.

- In 1955, while still working for Sun Studio, she returned to the air on WHER. The call letters were significant, because the station billed itself as "the Nation's First All-Girl Station." Keisker's voice was the first to be heard on WHER—just after midnight on Halloween, 1955, she gave the station's call letters, assigned frequency, and location.

- In 1957, a quarrel with Sam Phillips prompted her to quit her job and join the U.S. Air Force, where she received a commission. She eventually became a captain.

"...[Elvis] was like a mirror in a way: **whatever you were looking for, you were going to find in him.** It was not in him to lie or say anything malicious. He had all the intricacy of the very simple."

—Marion Keisker, **Last Train to Memphis** by Peter Guralnik

A Brand-New Sound

Elvis's first five records for Sun successfully integrated rhythm-and-blues with country and pop to produce rockabilly—one of the backbone sounds of rock 'n' roll.

1. *"That's All Right" and "Blue Moon of Kentucky"*
2. *"Good Rockin' Tonight" and "I Don't Care If the Sun Don't Shine"*
3. *"Milkcow Blues Boogie" and "You're a Heartbreaker"*
4. *"Baby Let's Play House" and "I'm Left, You're Right, She's Gone"*
5. *"Mystery Train" and "I Forgot to Remember to Forget"*

"That's All Right"

Elvis's first recording for Sun Records, "That's All Right," seemed to come about almost by accident. When Sam Phillips needed a singer to record a ballad called "Without You," he thought of Elvis Presley. Elvis had cut a couple of acetates at Phillips's Memphis Recording Service, and Phillips's assistant, Marion Keisker, had taped him for future reference. Phillips decided to let Elvis record "Without You," but the inexperienced singer wasn't able to master the song. Elvis sang several other tunes for Phillips, who put him together with guitarist Scotty Moore for some seasoning. Moore, Elvis, and Bill Black were working together at Sun on the evening of

July 5, 1954, trying to find a sound that clicked. Nothing seemed to be working. During a break, Elvis began singing Arthur "Big Boy" Crudup's country-blues tune "That's All Right" in a fast-paced, almost casual style. When Moore and Black jumped in, Phillips's voice boomed out from the control booth, "What are you doing?"

Phillips was excited by the trio's sound and recognized its potential. He recorded "That's All Right" that night and backed it a few days later with "Blue Moon of Kentucky." Elvis's approach to both songs differed from the originals. He used a more relaxed vocal style and higher key for "That's All Right" than Crudup had. He sped up the tempo for "Blue Moon of Kentucky" and omitted the high-pitched bluegrass singing style. Two elements were added to both songs that would make Elvis famous—syncopation and a "slapback" (electronically delayed) echo effect.

Arthur "Big Boy" Crudup

Dewey Phillips

Dewey Mills Phillips was a country boy from Adamsville, Tennessee, who came into his own on the airwaves of Memphis radio station WHBQ.

One of the many jobs he held after he blew into town was at the Taystee Bread Bakery, where he was fired for talking the bakers into halting production of bread loaves in order to make little bread people. As an employee of Grant's dime store, he created a sensation by playing records and talking like a deejay over the store's intercom. He finally succeeded in talking his way onto the staff of WHBQ, which broadcast from the Hotel Chisca. Phillips took control of the 15-minute music program "Red Hot and Blue." Within a year, the show expanded to three hours a day, with Dewey often showcasing the music of local rhythm-and-blues artists. Phillips had no formal training in radio, but his jive approach to announcing made him appealing to audiences.

Dewey, who was a close friend to Sam Phillips but no relation, was the first deejay to play Elvis's "That's All Right." In fact, he played it over and over. So many requests for the record came into the station that Dewey interviewed Elvis on the air on July 7, 1955.

By the late 1950s, hard times set in for the one-of-a-kind deejay. Top 40 programming quickly became the mainstay of popular radio, and personalities like Dewey Phillips were shoved aside. In and out of work over the next dozen years, Phillips never regained the stature he enjoyed in the early 1950s. In 1968, he died of pneumonia at age 42.

Dewey Phillips, Wink Martindale, and Elvis

On July 30, 1954, a hot summer night, Elvis made his first billed appearance at the *Overton Park Shell* in Memphis. The headliner was Slim Whitman, a country singer who incorporated yodeling into his style. Also on the bill were Billy Walker, Curly Harris, Sugarfoot Collins, Tinker Fry, and Sonny Harville. The newspaper ads promoting the event misspelled Elvis's name as "Ellis Presley." Elvis's first single, "That's All Right" backed by "Blue Moon of Kentucky," had been released just 11 days earlier, and most have speculated that he sang both songs that night. Elvis was clearly nervous for the first show, and he moved constantly while he was singing. The girls in the audience began to scream and make noise. After it was over, Elvis asked band member Scotty Moore what they were "hollering" at and Moore replied, "It was your leg, man. It was the way you were shakin' your left leg."

In August 1955, Elvis appeared with
Bill Strength at Overton Park Shell in Memphis.

"*While he appears with so-called hillbilly shows, Elvis's clothes are strictly sharp. His eyes are darkly slumbrous, his hair sleekly long, his sideburns low, and there is a lazy, sexy, tough, good-looking manner which bobby soxers like. Not all record stars go over as well on stage as they do on records.* **Elvis sells.**"

—*Robert Johnson,*
Memphis **Press-Scimitar***,*
February 5, 1955

"Some people tap their feet, some people snap their fingers, and some people sway back and forth. I just sorta do 'em all together, I guess."

—Elvis in 1956, talking about his way of moving on stage

The musicians who backed Elvis were essential to his sound in the 1950s. Elvis, guitarist Scotty Moore, and bassist Bill Black were dubbed the *Hillbilly Cat and the Blue Moon Boys.* Moore and Black hitched their wagons to Elvis's star after recording "That's All Right" with him. Moore's driving guitar sound helped create Elvis's style, while Black's antics on his upright bass added humor and excitement to their live act. After appearing with the group on *Louisiana Hayride,* drummer D. J. Fontana joined them on the road, although he never played on any of Elvis's Sun recordings. After Elvis became a household name, Moore, Black, and Fontana were not given the respect and salary they were due. Moore and Black split with Elvis in September 1957 over this issue. Both were wooed back, but things were never quite the same. Moore and Fontana recorded with Elvis after he returned from the army in 1960, but Black had already struck out on his own, enjoying moderate success with his own combo.

In the fall of 1954, Elvis was invited to perform on the *Grand Ole Opry*. On October 2, the Hillbilly Cat and the Blue Moon Boys drove from Memphis to Nashville to appear on the show. The audience was not enthusiastic. Because the *Opry* had always been reluctant to accept changes in country music, including the use of electric guitars and drums, it's not surprising that Elvis's highly charged performance of blues-inspired music was not appreciated.

"Maybe it's ironic that after that first appearance [on the *Grand Ole Opry*] the head of the *Opry* suggested that **Elvis try to find a day job,** and that Elvis cried all the way to Memphis after the *Opry* show. Then he went on to **become the biggest star** since Hank Williams. There's some kind of justice in that, I think."

—*Hank Williams Jr., reprinted in* Elvis! The Last Word, *1991*

On the Road, 1954–1955

Elvis appeared with a variety of country-western acts while under contract to Sun. Though his music did not sound like country, it was logical for him to tour the country circuits throughout the South. He toured with several singers who would become country music's biggest performers in the 1950s and 1960s, including Johnny Cash, Faron Young, Ferlin Huskey (later Husky), the Wilburn Brothers, Mother Maybelle and the Carter Sisters, Sonny James, Hank Locklin, Hank Snow, Webb Pierce, and the Louvin Brothers.

Johnny Cash with Elvis

"This cat came out in red pants and a green coat and a pink shirt and socks, and **he had this sneer on his face** and he stood behind the mike for five minutes, I'll bet, before he made a move. Then he hit his guitar a lick, and he broke two strings. So there he was, these two strings dangling . . . and these high school girls were **screaming and fainting** and running up to the stage, and then he started to move his hips real slow like he had a thing for his guitar."

—*Country singer Bob Luman*

In mid-October 1954, Elvis performed for the first time on *Louisiana Hayride*, a radio program broadcast from the Municipal Auditorium in Shreveport, Louisiana. *Hayride*, unlike the *Grand Ole Opry*, had always encouraged new country talent, including Hank Williams, Slim Whitman, Jim Reeves, and Webb Pierce. The Hillbilly Cat and the Blue Moon Boys sang "That's All Right" and "Blue Moon of Kentucky" during the "Lucky Strike Guest Time" segment, which was devoted to new artists. The trio was so well received that they were asked to return the next week. On November 6, *Louisiana Hayride* offered them a one-year contract to perform every weekend. The show paid scale wages, but it gave the trio valuable exposure to country fans outside of the Deep South.

"**[Elvis] was** *absolutely* **crazy about girls.** *He loved them—both figuratively and literally.... During that period in his life, I never saw Elvis take an alcoholic drink... I never saw him take so much as a puff from a regular cigarette, much less a marijuana cigarette. But he had an insatiable addiction to girls."*

—Horace Logan, talent coordinator
for **Louisiana Hayride**

"Why buy a cow when you can get milk through the fence?"

—*Elvis, when asked if he would marry, "Teener's Hero," Time, May 14, 1956*

SPOTLIGHT ON "Baby Let's Play House"

Elvis's fourth single for Sun Records, recorded on February 5, 1955, and released in late April, became his first effort to chart nationally. Backed by "I'm Left, You're Right, She's Gone" on the flip side, "Baby Let's Play House" stayed on *Billboard*'s country chart for ten weeks, reaching number ten.

Rhythm-and-blues singer Arthur Gunter wrote and recorded the song in 1954, basing it on country singer Eddy Arnold's 1951 hit, "I Want to Play House with You." A rhythm-and-blues reworking of a country-western song, "Baby Let's Play House" was perfect for Elvis's rockabilly repertoire. Gunter

Excellorec
BMI

Vocal
U-143

Baby Let's Play House
(Gunter)
ELVIS PRESLEY
SCOTTY & BILL
217
MEMPHIS, TENNESSEE

himself had been influenced by rockabilly artists, and he made a good model for Elvis, who had purchased a copy of Gunter's version the previous December at the House of Records in Memphis. Elvis made the song his own with the inclusion of the syncopated phrasing "Babe-babe-baby" in the verse. He also tinkered with the lyrics, changing "You may have religion" to "You may drive a pink Cadillac"—a humorous foretelling of the car he would come to be identified with. Sam Phillips added drums to the recording session for the song, marking the first time drums were used on an Elvis Presley single.

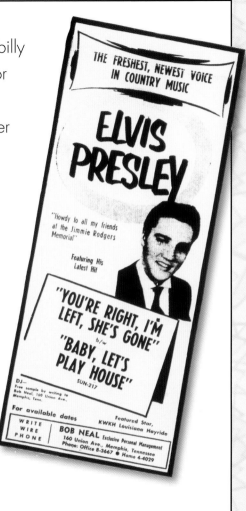

THE FRESHEST, NEWEST VOICE IN COUNTRY MUSIC

ELVIS PRESLEY

"Howdy to all my friends at the Jimmie Rodgers Memorial"

Featuring His Latest Hit

"YOU'RE RIGHT, I'M LEFT, SHE'S GONE"
b/w
"BABY, LET'S PLAY HOUSE"
SUN-217

DJ—
Free sample by writing to Bob Neal, 160 Union Ave., Memphis, Tenn.

For available dates

Featured Star, KWKH Louisiana Hayride

WRITE WIRE PHONE
BOB NEAL Exclusive Personal Management
160 Union Ave., Memphis, Tennessee
Phone: Office 8-3667 ● Home 4-4029

The Colonel

- Tom Parker was born Andreas Cornelis van Kuijk in Breda, Holland.

- Parker first saw Elvis in the spring of 1955 when Elvis was booked on a tour with country singer Hank Snow. The Colonel operated Snow's Jamboree Attractions.

- Parker's title of Colonel was not a military rank but an honorary title, which was bestowed on him by the state of Louisiana in 1953. In 1955, he was made an honorary Colonel of Tennessee.

- As a young man, Parker worked as a carnival barker and performer. Legend has it that as a carny, he painted sparrows yellow and sold them as parakeets.

- Elvis and the Colonel signed their first contract in August 1955, though Bob Neal was Elvis's official manager. By March 15, 1956, Neal was completely out of the picture, and the Colonel was Elvis's sole manager.

"*People say the Colonel has a good thing in me. Sure he has. And I've got a good thing in him.*"

—*Elvis*

"I'd rather try and **close a deal with the devil.**"

—Film producer
*Hal Wallis commenting on
the Colonel*

In November 1955, Sam Phillips sold Elvis's contract to *RCA Victor* for $35,000, plus $5,000 in back royalties he owed Elvis. It was the largest amount paid for a single performer up to that time. Steve Sholes, RCA's premier A&R (artist and repertoire) executive, had helped sign Elvis to the label. Sholes oversaw the company's specialty singles, which included country-western, gospel, and rhythm-and-blues, so he served as the producer of Elvis's first recordings for RCA. Moving to RCA was a major step in Elvis's career and a major investment for the company; at the very least, it meant going national and international in promotion and distribution. Sholes was aware that executives at RCA were closely watching their unusual new artist, who didn't fit into any of the company's existing categories of music.

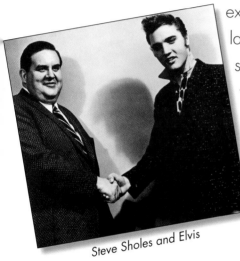

Steve Sholes and Elvis

RCA re-released Elvis's Sun singles in December 1955, then the company arranged for Elvis to begin recording new material in

Nashville the next month. In his first session for RCA, which began on January 10, 1956, Elvis recorded "I Got a Woman," "Heartbreak Hotel," "Money Honey," "I'm Counting on You," and "I Was the One." Steve Sholes was disconcerted by Elvis's off-handed, instinctual approach to recording, in which he sang a take, played it back, discarded it, and then sang another, repeating the process until he felt he had captured the tune. Elvis did not read music, nor did he

Elvis records for RCA.

have any professional experience at arranging it. He just instinctively knew what to do and when to do it. RCA executives in New York were also troubled by the Nashville session. The recordings did not sound as much like Elvis's Sun records as they had wanted, and the two ballads were nothing like his previous releases.

"Heartbreak Hotel"

ELVIS PRESLEY

HEARTBREAK HOTEL

and
I WAS THE ONE

"I walk a lonely street." So read the suicide note of an anonymous soul who ended his life in a Miami hotel. *The Miami Herald* ran a photo of his corpse on the front page with the headline, "Do You Know This Man?" The story went on to explain that the man had been discovered with no identification. Police found only the note in one of his pockets.

In Gainesville, songwriter-musician Tommy Durden thought the line in the note resonated the blues and would make a great lyric in a song. He sought the opinion of his friend Mae Boren Axton, who was a local songwriter, TV personality, and publicist.

Axton had once done some work for Colonel Tom Parker, and she suggested that they write the song for Elvis Presley. As the story goes, Axton had once told Elvis that she was going to write his first million seller. After Mae decided that "down at the end of Lonely Street" one would naturally find a "Heartbreak Hotel," the rest of the song was composed by the team within the hour. Glen Reeves, a local singer, recorded a demo record of the song in a style that suggested Elvis Presley. Axton flew to Nashville in November 1955 to introduce the song to Elvis. Elvis loved the song, supposedly exclaiming, "Hot dog, Mae!" as he played it about ten times in a row.

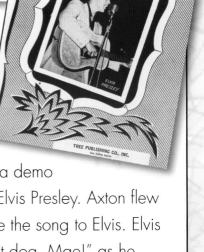

When Elvis charged in front of the cameras for the first time on *Tommy and Jimmy Dorsey's Stage Show* on January 28, 1956, he began a love-hate relationship with the television industry that kept his name in the headlines for most of that year. He returned to *Stage Show* on February 4, February 11, February 18, March 17, and March 24.

Rock 'n' roller Elvis and big-band leaders Tommy and Jimmy Dorsey represented popular music from two different eras.

The major problem with Elvis in the eyes of authority figures was the way he used his performing style to whip his largely female audiences into a frenzy during his concert performances. His gyrating pelvis, leg movements, and continual motion were considered far too provocative for mainstream audiences. Sometime during 1956, Elvis was dubbed *"Elvis the Pelvis,"* a nickname he despised.

The press almost always described an Elvis concert as mass hysteria, paying particular attention to the manner in which the girls screamed and cried uncontrollably. At times, the crowds stormed the stage to get to Elvis, who urged them on by leaning over the stage toward the crowd until he was almost—almost—close enough to touch. Police were assigned to surround the area just below the stage to keep the crowds away from him. Focusing on the hysteria generated by his performing style, newspaper stories painted Elvis as a catalyst for misbehavior among his fans.

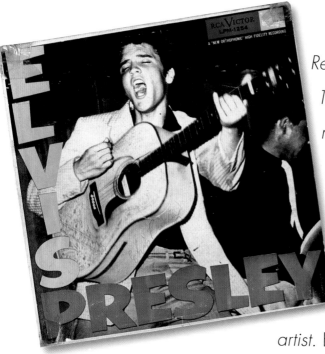

Released on March 13, 1956, *Elvis Presley* sold more than 360,000 copies by the end of April. At $3.98 per album, this made it **RCA's first million-dollar album** by a single artist. *Elvis Presley* also became the first album in music history to sell more than a million copies. It reached No. 1 on Billboard's Top LPs chart.

ELVIS PRESLEY

Side One
Heartbreak Hotel
I Was The One
Blue Suede Shoes
I'm Counting On You
I Got A Woman
One-Sided Love Affair
I Love You Because
Just Because
Tutti Frutti

Side Two
Trying To Get To You
I'm Gonna Sit Right Down And Cry (Over You)
I'll Never Let You Go (Little Darlin')
Blue Moon
Money Honey
Shake, Rattle And Roll
My Baby Left Me
Lawdy, Miss Clawdy
I Want You, I Need You, I Love You

Compilation Produced by
Ernst Mikael Jørgensen and **Roger Semon**
Original Engineer: **Sam Phillips,**
Bob Ferris and **Ernie Oehlrich**
Executive Directors: **Mike Omansky**
and **Klaus Schmalenbach**
Project Director: **Dalila Keumurian**

Elvis Presley zoomed into big-time entertainment practically overnight. Born in Tupelo, Mississippi, Elvis began singing for friends and folk gatherings when he was barely five years old. All his training has been self-instruction and hard work. At an early age, with not enough money to buy a guitar, he practiced for his future stardom by strumming on a broomstick. He soon graduated to a $2.98 instrument and began picking out tunes and singing on street corners.

After earning some money by working at part-time jobs, Elvis walked into a small recording company studio and asked to make a record, at his own expense. In a few months his first record was released and became an overnight sensation. Following his graduation from high school, Elvis began an extended round of personal appearances and then signed his contract with RCA Victor. The rest is history.

Elvis is the most original protagonist of popular songs on the scene today. His style stands out vividly on records and in personal appearances and accounts for the universal popularity he has gained.

"I lose myself in my singing. Maybe it's my early training singing gospel hymns. I'm limp as a rag, worn out when a show's over."

—*Elvis*, Tacoma New Tribune,
September 2, 1957

"I wiggle my shoulders, I shake my legs, I walk up and down the stage, I hop around on one foot. **But I never bump and grind.** *Why,* ***that's vulgar.*** I'd never do anything vulgar before an audience. My mother would never allow it."

—*Elvis*

The controversy over Elvis's sensual performing style reached a fever pitch during his 1956 summer tour. When Elvis played Jacksonville, Florida, in mid-August, he sold out all three shows for both nights at the *Florida Theater.* Reacting to the publicity surrounding "Elvis the Pelvis," Juvenile Court Judge Marion W. Gooding attended the first show, in which Elvis moved to his music as usual. Gooding met with Elvis and Colonel Tom Parker afterward and warned the young singer to "quieten" his act. The police attended to film the show to ensure that Elvis obeyed the judge's directive. In an atypical display of sarcasm, Elvis reacted to the directive by wiggling only his little finger during the performance. *LIFE* magazine centered its August 27 article on Elvis around the Jacksonville incident, sensationalizing the stories about the judge's threats and the tales about the crazed fans who tore off Elvis's clothes after one of his shows.

"He's just one big hunk of forbidden fruit."

—Teenage girl to songwriter Mae Boren Axton

"In a pivoting stance, his hips swing sensuously from side to side and his entire body takes on a frantic quiver, as if he had swallowed a jackhammer."

—Time, May 15, 1956

The Jordanaires

This gospel quartet has backed a diverse range of performers since it was formed in 1948, including Kitty Wells, Hank Snow, and Ricky Nelson. The group's lineup has changed several times over the years. The four men who backed Elvis Presley were Hoyt Hawkins (baritone), Gordon Stoker (first tenor), Hugh Jarrett (bass), and Neal Matthews (second tenor). In January 1956, Stoker was included as a backup singer on Elvis's first RCA recording session in a makeshift group with Ben and Brock Speer of the gospel-singing Speer Family. On another session later that year, Stoker was again hired to back Elvis without the rest of the quartet. When Elvis asked where the rest of the Jordanaires were, Stoker replied that he had been the only one asked. Elvis reportedly told him, "If anything comes of this, I want the Jordanaires to work all my sessions from now on, and my personal appearances, too." With that verbal agreement, the Jordanaires became "the Sound Behind the King" for more than a decade.

Elvis with the Jordanaires

Vegas Flop

In April 1956, the Colonel booked Elvis for a *two-week engagement* at the New Frontier Hotel in Las Vegas, a venture that *turned out to be a disaster.* Perhaps Parker should have known better than to book Elvis for a major engagement outside of the South with an audience made up mostly of adults. After a few performances, Elvis was bumped to second billing in favor of a more typical Vegas entertainer, comedian Shecky Green. Stung by the rejection, Elvis would remember his failure in Las Vegas for many years.

However, Elvis did have a stroke of luck during the Vegas trip: He was introduced to "Hound Dog" when he saw Freddie Bell and the Bellboys perform the song in the hotel lounge. A few months later, "Hound Dog" became Elvis's signature song, ultimately bringing him as much controversy as fame.

Right: *Elvis in Las Vegas, 1956.*
Inset: *Elvis mugs in a 25-cent photo booth.*

Most Controversial Television Appearance

- The television appearance that generated the most controversy was when Elvis appeared on *The Milton Berle Show* on June 5, 1956.

- His highly charged performance of "Hound Dog" caused the commotion.

- For the climax of "Hound Dog," Elvis slowed down the tempo to repeat the song's chorus. While belting out the final verse to a blues beat, he turned his body in profile and thrust his pelvis at the microphone. Elvis rested his hand next to the crotch of his pants, which emphasized the provocative connotation of the movement.

- This was Elvis's second appearance on the Berle show; he had appeared on April 3, when the show originated from the aircraft carrier U.S.S. *Hancock*.

"When I first knew Elvis, he had a million dollars worth of talent. Now he has a million dollars."

—Colonel Tom Parker, 1956

"My fans **want my shirt,** *they* **can have my shirt.**

They put it on my back."

—*Elvis,* Illustrated, *September 7, 1957*

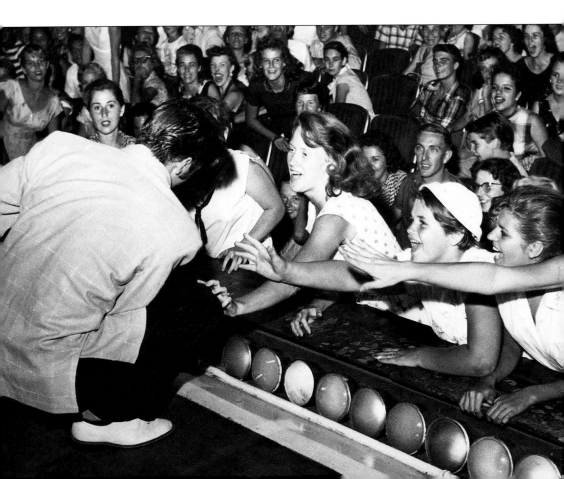

"Hound Dog"

After Elvis rocked *The Milton Berle Show* with his bump-and-grind rendition of "Hound Dog," the gritty rhythm-and-blues tune became indelibly linked with the performer. The song was written by Jerry Leiber and Mike Stoller in 1952 for blues singer Willie Mae "Big Mama" Thornton. Several performers covered "Hound Dog," including country artists Tommy Duncan, Betsy Gay, Jack Turner, and Billy Starr, and lounge act Freddie Bell and the Bellboys. Bell enlivened the tempo and tampered with the lyrics in a humorous way, adding the line, "You ain't never caught a rabbit, and you ain't no friend of mine." Elvis caught the Bellboys' act in April 1956 when he was booked into the New Frontier Hotel in Las Vegas. Though Elvis and his combo flopped in Vegas, he brought back a little souvenir in the form of Bell's comedic version of "Hound Dog."

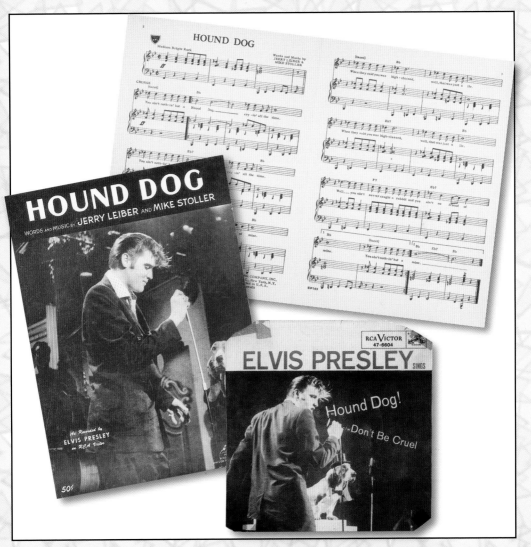

Respected singer-songwriter *Otis Blackwell* composed many rock 'n' roll standards in the 1950s and 1960s. Born in Brooklyn in 1932, Blackwell grew up admiring country-western singer and actor Tex Ritter. He became a staff writer for Shalimar Music in early 1956 after he sold six songs, including "Don't Be Cruel," for $25 each to that company. Blackwell had been standing in front of the Brill Building (home to rock 'n' roll music publishing) in New York City on Christmas Eve when an arranger asked him if he had any songs to sell. The man then took Blackwell to meet Shalimar's owners, who purchased the songs and hired him after the holidays. Elvis recorded ten Blackwell compositions, including "Fever" (written with Eddie Cooley), "All Shook Up," "Paralyzed," and "Return to Sender" (cowritten with Winfield Scott). Among Blackwell's other rock 'n' roll classics are Jerry Lee Lewis's "Great Balls of Fire" and "Breathless." Blackwell sang on the demos of his songs for Elvis and Jerry Lee and imitated their styles, but he and Elvis never met.

Myth vs. Fact

During Elvis's final appearance on *The Ed Sullivan Show* on January 6, 1957, the cameras shot the provocative singer only from the waist up. Speculation runs rampant as to why Sullivan and the censors chose to take this approach. The most common explanation is that Sullivan had received negative feedback from Elvis's previous performances. Another explanation is offered by Dave Marsh in his biography *Elvis*. He hints that Sullivan's actions were a reaction to the antics of the Colonel, who had supposedly forced the TV host to apologize on-air for negative remarks he had made about Elvis. Jane and Michael Stern offer a humorous but dubious explanation in their book *Elvis World*. In this version, Elvis had put a cardboard tube down his pants during his October appearance and manipulated it in an overtly sexual way. To avoid a repeated occurrence, Sullivan ordered the above-the-waist coverage.

*"I'll **not have him at any price**—he's not my cup of tea."*

—Ed Sullivan before Elvis's ratings-busting performance on **The Steve Allen Show,** July 23, 1956

"I want to say to **Elvis Presley** and the country that **this is a real decent boy,** and we've never had a pleasanter experience on our show with a big name than we've had with you."

—Ed Sullivan after Elvis's third appearance on **The Ed Sullivan Show,** January 6, 1957

At the request of Colonel Tom Parker, famed Hollywood clothing designer Nudie Cohen created a *gold lamé suit* for Elvis for his 1957 tours. It consisted of gold slacks and a jacket woven from spun gold thread. Cohen had established a reputation among country music stars for creating brightly colored western-style costumes with elaborate embroidery. While colorful stage attire was typical of country performers, the mainstream press simply was not ready for Elvis and his glittering raiment, and they used its conspicuous nature to attack Elvis. As the tour progressed, the reported cost of the suit grew higher and higher. The St. Louis *Post-Dispatch* claimed it cost $2,500; the Fort Wayne *News Sentinel* reported that the jacket alone cost $2,000; by the time Elvis crossed the border, Canadian papers valued the suit at $4,000. Elvis never liked his gold lamé suit because it was heavy and uncomfortable. After ripping the pants during a performance, *he never wore the entire suit again.*

Graceland

- Graceland was built in 1939 by Dr. Thomas Moore and named after his wife's aunt, Grace Toof.

- Elvis purchased Graceland in March 1957 for slightly more than $100,000. The house was located on 13.8 acres of land.

- After the purchase, Elvis renovated the house and then made several additions over the years until Graceland consisted of 23 rooms, and the grounds included the Trophy Room and Meditation Garden, where Elvis is buried, as well as a carport, bathhouse, and racquetball court.

- Graceland was opened to the public in 1982, placed on the National Register of Historic Places in 1991, and declared a National Historic Landmark in 2006.

Best Elvis Collectibles: 1950s

Elvis Presley Lipsticks. Merchandiser Hank Saperstein made a deal with the Colonel to market Elvis's image on about 30 products, including lipstick. Shades included Hound Dog Orange, Heartbreak Pink, Cruel Red, and Tutti Frutti Red.

Elvis Presley Sneakers. Two different colors of sneakers were available, a green and black pair and a black and white pair.

Elvis Presley Underwear. After the Saperstein deal, fans could literally dress themselves from head to toe in Elvis, but the underwear must have generated the most interest.

Teddy Bear Perfume. Teen-Age, Inc., came up with Teddy Bear Eau de Parfum, inspired by Elvis's 1957 hit single "Teddy Bear." The tall, slender bottle featured a photo of Elvis from the 1950s. Collectors should beware of the reissue from the 1960s, which features a later photo of Elvis.

The Pink Items. In 1956, Elvis Presley Enterprises issued an autograph book, diary, scrapbook, photo album, and record case as a set of must-have accessories for every teenage girl. All of the items were dusty pink and featured the same black line drawing of Elvis.

Teenzines

Among the most delightful of all magazines about Elvis are the teenzines from the mid-to-late 1950s, because they cover the burgeoning days of rock 'n' roll. One of the most sought-after single-issue magazines is *Elvis Presley: Hero or Heel?* Another is *Elvis Answers Back*, which included a 78 rpm flexi disc recording with Elvis's voice. Regularly issued teenzines of the era included *Dig* and *Hep Cats*.

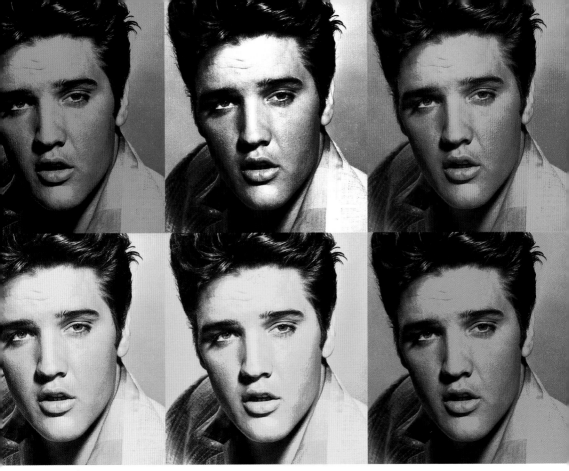

"Before Elvis, everything was in black and white. Then came Elvis. Zoom, **glorious Technicolor.***"

—*Keith Richards*

In the Army Now

- Elvis was inducted on March 28, 1958, and got his famous army haircut at Fort Chaffee, Arkansas.

- His serial number was 53310761.

- Elvis took basic training at Fort Hood, Texas.

- He served two years in the Third Armored Division in Bad Nauheim, West Germany.

- Just before coming home in 1960, Elvis met 14-year-old Priscilla Beaulieu, whom he dated for the rest of his tour in the army.

- Elvis arrived home on March 3, 1960. At a press conference at Fort Dix, New Jersey, Nancy Sinatra was there to greet the singer bearing gifts from her father, Frank Sinatra.

- Elvis was officially discharged from the army on March 5. His final paycheck was $109.54.

Flaming Star:
A Hollywood Leading Man

"A **Presley picture** is the *only* **sure thing** in Hollywood."

—*Producer Hal Wallis*

Nothing incites more disagreement among biographers, fans, and music critics than Elvis Presley's career as a *leading man* in Hollywood movies. Often blamed for a perceived decline in his music, the movies are generally disliked and harshly criticized by biographers and rock 'n' roll fans. Elvis himself disliked the musical comedies he made and was disappointed that he was unable to stretch his acting abilities in other genres.

However, an updated consideration of his films results in an alternative view. While most of Elvis's musicals are not classics, he certainly appeared in more well-crafted films than most pop performers of the period. Furthermore, none of his movies lost money for the studios that financed them, and, in retrospect, they offer wholesome entertainment that is in keeping with the traditional musical. Some of the songs and production numbers were poorly written and conceived, but some of his movie tunes became pop classics, with several currently enjoying a revival. Viewed today, many of the production numbers have a campy appeal that offers insight into the fads and trends of another era.

ELVIS'S FIRST *Film*

Love Me Tender

In this drama set immediately after the Civil War, Elvis costars as Clint, the youngest son in the Reno family. This was the only time in his acting career that Elvis played a secondary role.

Elvis's first experience as a Hollywood actor was closely followed in the entertainment press from the day he was assigned a role in *Love Me Tender* until the day the film was released. The close scrutiny affected the outcome of the film in several ways. Originally called *The Reno Brothers*, this western drama was retitled after a number of articles announced that advance sales for "Love Me Tender"—one of the songs recorded for the film—exceeded a million copies. It was the first time advance sales for a single release had ever surpassed the million mark, and the producers capitalized on the publicity by changing the film's title.

The enormous amount of press coverage also affected the film's conclusion. During production, fanzines leaked that Elvis's character was supposed to die near the end of the film. As originally shot, the final scene features Mother Reno solemnly ringing the dinner bell as her three remaining sons toil in the fields. Pain and loss are registered on the faces

of Mother Reno and Cathy, who mourn the death of Clint. Elvis's legion of fans was disturbed by the news that their idol was to be killed off in his first film. In an attempt to counter an "adverse public reaction," 20th Century-Fox shot an alternative ending in which Clint is spared. This second ending was rejected, and a compromise ending was used instead. Clint is killed as called for in the original script, but the final shot superimposed a ghostly close-up of Elvis as Clint crooning "Love Me Tender" as his family slowly walks away from his grave. The fans were then left with a final image of Elvis doing what he was famous for—singing.

Movie Dialogue

Clint (Elvis):
Whoa!...
Brett...Vance...
They told us you
were dead!

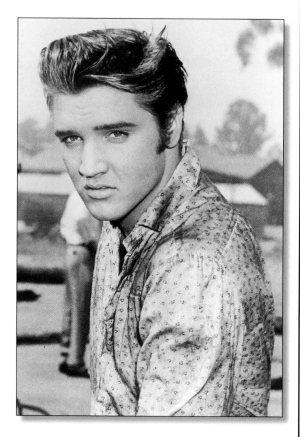

"That boy could *charm the birds from the trees.* He was so eager and humble, we went out of our way to help him."

—*Richard Egan, who played older brother Vance Reno in* Love Me Tender

Panned in the Press

Some of the reviews for Elvis's performance in **Love Me Tender** were brutal, though many critics seemed prejudiced by the negative press over his controversial performing style as a singer.

"**Is it a sausage?** It is certainly smooth and damp-looking.... Is it a Walt Disney goldfish? It has the same sort of big, soft, beautiful eyes and long, curly lashes....**Is it a corpse?** The face just hangs there, limp and white with its little drop-seat mouth, rather like Lord Byron in the wax museum."

—Time

"*Love Me Tender* will have no place in motion picture history, but it may very well have a place in the history of American morals and mores, for Presley is a pied piper who could lead his followers to an end more socially deleterious than their permanent disappearance in a cave." —*Henry Hart*, Films in Review

"...in a magnificent death scene...oddly, he reminds one of Liberace."

—*Hollis Alpert,* The Saturday Review

"Appraising Presley *as an actor, he ain't.* Not that it makes much difference. The presence of Presley apparently is enough to satisfy the juve [juvenile] set."   —**Variety**

SPOTLIGHT ON *Loving You*

Elvis Presley was not simply the star of *Loving You;* in a sense, he was also the subject. The film served as a vehicle built around Elvis's image and was designed to showcase his rock 'n' roll music and explosive performing style. The storyline, costuming, and music incorporated specific characteristics strongly associated with the real-life Elvis Presley and then manipulated them to suit specific ends. The ultimate effect was a reshaping of Elvis's rebel image into one more recognizable and therefore more acceptable to mainstream audiences.

Some of Elvis's family and friends appear in Loving You *in cameos and bit parts. His parents, Gladys and Vernon, appear as members of the audience in the final production number. Real-life band members Scotty Moore, Bill Black, and D. J. Fontana have bit parts as Elvis's bandmates.*

The "Teddy Bear" Costume

Elvis's purported fondness for teddy bears was likely just a publicity stunt manufactured by the Colonel in the 1950s. One offshoot of the story holds that Kal Mann and Bernie Lowe composed the song "Teddy Bear" for Elvis supposedly as a response to the rumors. Elvis performed the song in his second film, *Loving You*, which was shot in glorious Technicolor. The cinematography, with its rich, saturated colors, proved the perfect vehicle to exploit the film's 1950s-style costumes. For the "Teddy Bear" number, Elvis wore a silky, maroon and white, western-style outfit. The engaging love song combined with the endearing ensemble served to soften Elvis's rebellious persona. Aside from being a fan favorite, the costume gained attention when it was discussed on *You Bet Your*

Life, a television game show hosted by Groucho Marx. The president of the San Diego Elvis Presley Fan Club, who had purchased the costume, appeared on the show, and Groucho teased her about her passion for Elvis and her unusual acquisition.

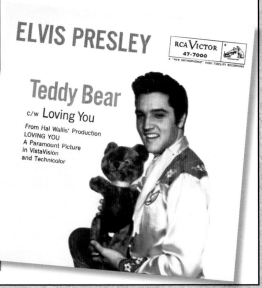

ELVIS'S FIRST *Kiss*

Elvis received his **first passionate on-screen kiss** *in his second feature,* Loving You. *Actress Jana Lund bestowed the legendary kiss, which was the one act that made her minor screen career memorable. Other films she appeared in included the teen flicks* Don't Knock the Rock, High School Hellcats, *and* Hot Car Girl. *Her last screen appearance was in* Married Too Young *in 1962.*

SPOTLIGHT ON Jailhouse Rock

King Creole boasts a powerful cast and a skilled director, and *Blue Hawaii* features slick production values, but the gritty, low-budget *Jailhouse Rock* remains Elvis Presley's best film. Elvis, the rock 'n' roll rebel, liberated a generation from the values, tastes, and ideals of their parents, and *Jailhouse Rock* is the only Presley film that speaks directly to the feral, sensual, and unruly nature of rock 'n' roll music.

The heart of *Jailhouse Rock* is the character of Vince Everett, who swaggers and prowls through the film with attitude and magnetism. Despite his Hollywood-style conversion in the final moments, it is Vince's impudence and haughty defiance that stay with the viewer long after the final fadeout. The character embodies the rebellious spirit of rock 'n' roll, in much the same way that Elvis did in his career. This close identification between real-life performer and fictional character is not a detriment; indeed, it is the film's strength.

Favorite Dialogue from Elvis Flicks

Peggy: How dare you think that cheap tactics would work with me?

Vince (Elvis): Them ain't tactics honey. That's just the beast in me!

—Jailhouse Rock

Jailhouse Rock's most famous production number was
choreographed by Alex Romero.

Myth vs. Fact

The scene in which the prison barber shaves off Elvis's infamous ducktail made fans weep and parents cheer. Over the years, much speculation existed as to whether it was Elvis's *real hair* that was cut **or a wig.** A glance at the production schedule as reprinted in Jim Hannaford's *Inside Jailhouse Rock* reveals the truth: Two wigs were used to represent Elvis's atrocious prison 'do. The schedule indicates that Elvis had to film three scenes in one week—one with the butch haircut, one with the hair partially grown back, and one with his regular style. Obviously, his real hair could not have grown back in that short span of time. In later years, makeup artist William Tuttle revealed that a series of plaster casts of Elvis's head allowed them to make wigs that fit so well that they were nearly impossible to detect.

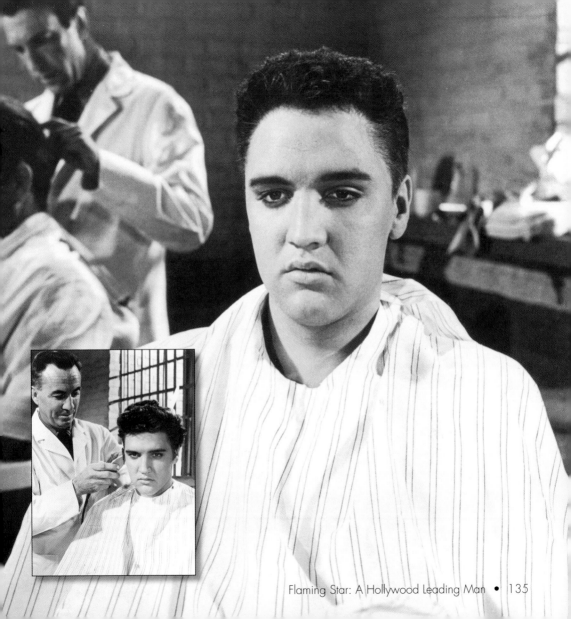

Penned by the legendary Jerry Leiber and Mike Stoller, *"Jailhouse Rock"* became another big hit for Elvis. It entered the British charts at number one, making it the first U.S. single ever to do so. The rock 'n' roll songwriting duo was commissioned to write most of the songs from the movie *Jailhouse Rock,* though they were less than enthusiastic about the assignment.

During the April 1957 recording session for "Jailhouse Rock," Leiber and Stoller quickly changed their minds about Elvis when they realized he knew his music and that he was a workhorse in the studio. The pair took over the recording sessions, serving as unofficial producers of "Jailhouse Rock," "Treat Me Nice," "(You're So Square) Baby, I Don't Care," and other tunes. Their collaboration with Elvis and his musicians on "Jailhouse Rock" resulted in the singer's hardest-rocking movie song. As D. J. Fontana once noted about his drum playing on the record, "I tried to think of someone on a chain gang smashing rocks."

Great Movie Tunes

"Love Me Tender" from *Love Me Tender*

"Teddy Bear" from *Loving You*

"Mean Woman Blues" from *Loving You*

"(You're So Square) Baby, I Don't Care" from *Jailhouse Rock*

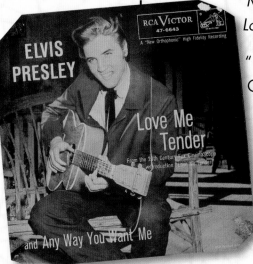

"Treat Me Nice" from Jailhouse Rock

"Trouble" from King Creole

"New Orleans" from King Creole

"Hard Headed Woman" from King Creole

"G. I. Blues" from G. I. Blues

Hal B. Wallis
The Man Who Believed Elvis Could Act

Hal Wallis, a respected veteran of the film industry, worked in Hollywood from the silent era through the 1970s. He began as a publicity representative for Warner Brothers, working his way up to executive producer in charge of production by 1933. There he produced several classics, including *Little Caesar, Sergeant York*, and *The Maltese Falcon*. In 1944, he became an independent producer, releasing his films through Paramount and later Universal. As an independent, Wallis had a reputation for fostering new talent and was dubbed "the Discoverer." Among those whose screen careers he helped were Kirk Douglas, the team of Dean Martin and Jerry Lewis, Shirley MacLaine, and Elvis Presley.

Of the nine films that Wallis produced starring Elvis, Wallis's personal favorite was *King Creole*. He once said that one of the biggest regrets in his career was that he was not able to follow through on his idea for a western starring John Wayne as an older gunfighter with Elvis as his protégé. Wallis died in 1986.

"When I ran the test, I felt the same thrill I experienced when I first saw Errol Flynn on the screen. *Elvis,* in a very different, modern way, had exactly the same *power, virility, and sexual drive.* The camera caressed him."

—*Hal Wallis, Starmaker, on Elvis's screen test*

King Creole *was considered a major Hollywood production. Director Michael Curtiz (far left) and producer Hal Wallis confer with Elvis behind the scenes.*

"Anybody who will **pay my boy a million dollars** can make any kind of [motion] picture they want."

—*Colonel Tom Parker, 1960s*

King Creole

A musical drama with a cast of Hollywood's most respected character actors, *King Creole* was directed by veteran Michael Curtiz and produced by Hal Wallis for Paramount Pictures. Though not a classic, it is a well-crafted example of a typical Hollywood film from the era when the studio system still dominated the industry. In this production, which was less of a vehicle designed around Elvis than the majority of his movies were, the young actor held his own with a cast of talented professionals. *King Creole* now stands as a testament to Elvis's acting potential, which was never fully realized in the succession of teen musicals he made in the 1960s.

Elvis worked with a number of talented character actors and veteran movie stars throughout his career, but he rarely had a supporting cast of the caliber of *King Creole*. Some of the cast members were at the peak of their careers; some were established supporting players who had been a part of Hollywood for several years; some were relative unknowns at the start of lucrative careers. Elvis's stellar costars on this film included Carolyn Jones, Walter Matthau, Dolores Hart, Dean Jagger, and Vic Morrow.

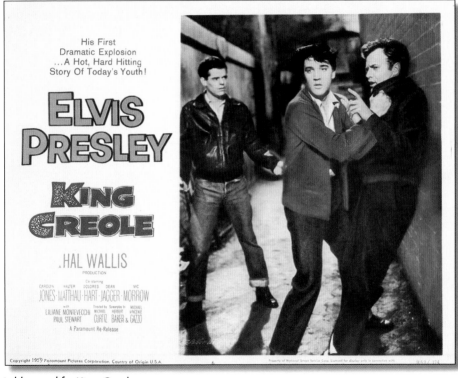

Lobby card for King Creole

"He was an instinctive actor.... He was quite bright.... *He was not a punk.* He was very elegant, sedate, and refined, and sophisticated."

—*Walter Matthau, on costarring with Elvis in* King Creole, *1987 interview*

"He's the **best-mannered star** in Hollywood, and he's improved as a performer and has determination to be a fine actor. [Elvis] was smart enough to simmer down that torrid act of his."

—Hedda Hopper,
early 1960s

On his return from the army in 1960, Elvis was scheduled to appear on *Welcome Home, Elvis,* a television special hosted by Frank Sinatra. Frank sent his daughter Nancy to the airport as Elvis's official greeter. The pair struck up a friendship that lasted for years and provided sparkling chemistry in *Speedway.* Her version of "Your Groovy Self" was included on the soundtrack album, marking the only time another artist sang a solo on a regular RCA Elvis album. In the mid–1960s, Nancy recorded four hit duets with singer-

Elvis and Nancy

songwriter Lee Hazlewood, who also wrote her best-known hit, "These Boots Are Made for Walking." Nancy earned her third gold record for a duet she sang with her father, "Something Stupid." She also spent a large part of the 1960s cavorting through teen musicals such as *Get Yourself a College Girl* (1964) and *The Ghost in the Invisible Bikini* (1966). During the mid–1990s, Nancy rode the crest of a nostalgia wave, singing her 1960s hits to a new generation and appearing in *Playboy* magazine.

"He is no longer the sneering, hip-twitching symbol of the untamed beast that resides in 17-year-old breasts. He has come back from the Army easygoing, unassuming..."

—Life, October 10, 1960

SpotLight on G.I. Blues

In May 1960, Elvis had returned to Hollywood to begin shooting *G.I. Blues*. The movie's storyline is about a singer serving in the army in Germany. Producer Hal Wallis borrowed details from Elvis's own life to flesh out the script just as he had done in the two previous films he made with Elvis. In *G.I. Blues*, Elvis's character is not only stationed in Germany, he's also a member of a tank division just as Elvis had been.

Like the movies Elvis made before going into the army, *G.I. Blues* is based on the events of his own life, but it is a musical comedy instead of a musical drama. *G.I. Blues* was aimed at a family audience, and Elvis's controversial performing style was toned down. Even though most of the songs are fast-paced, they don't have the same hard-driving sound, sexual connotation, or emotional delivery of Elvis's prior soundtrack recordings. Elvis's screen image was deliberately softened for *G.I. Blues*. In one scene, he sings a Bavariansounding folk tune during a children's puppet show, while in another he baby-sits an adorable infant. The movie's ads perfectly sum up these changes: "See and Hear the New Elvis: The Idol of Teenagers Is the Idol of the Family."

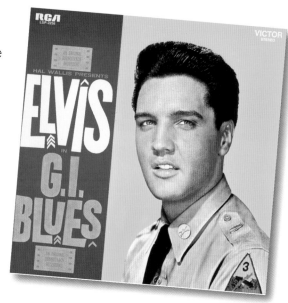

G.I. Blues was enormously successful, ranking 14th in box-office receipts for 1960. Movie critics applauded the new Elvis. They approved of his new image and predicted he would find plenty of new fans among older women. Elvis didn't share the critics' enthusiasm for *G.I. Blues*. He felt that there were too many musical numbers and believed some of them made no sense within the context of the plot. He was concerned that the quality of many of these songs was not as good as the music from his earlier movies.

Favorite Dialogue from Elvis Flicks

Maile (soaking wet): I bought this dress to welcome you home. It's the first time I've worn it.

Chad (Elvis): You know something? On you, wet is my favorite color.

—Blue Hawaii

Much of *Blue Hawaii* was filmed on location in America's 50th state, which had only joined the union in 1959. Such beautiful Hawaiian locations as Waikiki Beach, Ala Moana Park, Lydgate Park, and the Coco Palms Resort Hotel were used in the film.

Blue Hawaii

"Exciting romance . . . Dances . . . Music in the World's Lushest Paradise of Song!" "Elvis Presley Guides You Through a Paradise of Song!" So blared the promotion for *Blue Hawaii*, Elvis's most financially successful film. Its lush location footage, large selection of songs, and colorful supporting cast accounted for its popularity, success, and good reputation, and that success and popularity determined

Elvis plays a singing tour guide in Blue Hawaii.

the course of Elvis's movie career thereafter. With *Blue Hawaii,* a formula was established for Presley vehicles that was followed almost exclusively for the rest of his career. Exotic locales and vacation settings—

Elvis and Joan Blackman marry in a Hawaiian wedding ceremony in the beautiful final sequence of Blue Hawaii.

and the romance and escape that went with them—became such well-known elements in certain Elvis movies that he disparagingly dubbed them the "Presley travelogues."

"Can't Help Falling in Love"

Written specifically for *Blue Hawaii* by George Weiss, Hugo Peretti, and Luigi Creatore, "Can't Help Falling in Love" is remembered as the ballad with which Elvis closed his concerts during the 1970s. In the film, Elvis's character sings it to his girlfriend's grandmother for her birthday, but that context has long since been forgotten. Because Elvis sang it so many times in concert, it is more fitting to suggest that the song belongs to the fans. It speaks to the way the fans felt about Elvis, and it was his love song to them.

Record collectors should note that the movie version of "Can't Help Falling in Love" was not the one released as a single or on the album. Two takes of the movie version were recorded along with one take of the single release. The movie version of "Can't Help Falling in Love" was not released until after Elvis's death.

In his musical comedies, Elvis often broke into song at any time, a characteristic he hated about his films. Here, he sings "Island of Love (Kauai)" to a tour group.

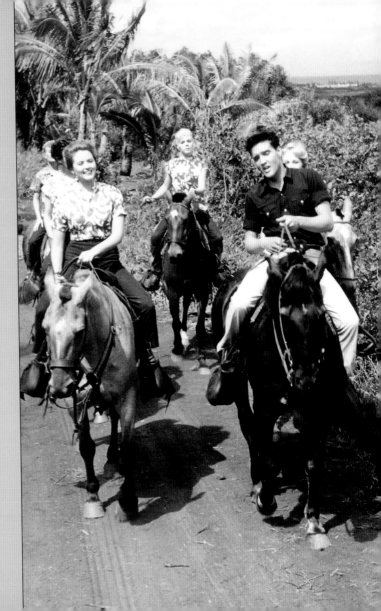

What's in a Name?

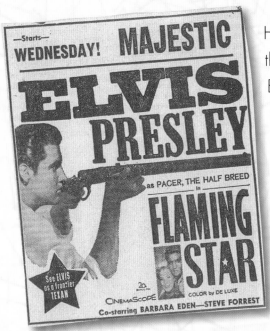

Hollywood films commonly change their titles during production, but Elvis's musical comedies were notorious for doing this, often at the very last minute. Sometimes the change represented an improvement, as when *Hawaii Beach Boy* was given the much more romantic title *Blue Hawaii*. Usually, however, the final titles were little better than the originals. *Flaming Star* was at various times *Flaming Lance, Flaming Heart,* and *Black Star. In My Harem* became *Harem Holiday,* which turned into *Harem Scarum* and then finally *Harum Scarum,* with that all-important misspelling so that the first word could match the second. The memorable *Kiss My Firm But Pliant Lips* was

Live a Little, Love a Little

Spinout

changed to the forgettable
*Live a Little, Love a Little. A Girl in Every
Port* became *Welcome Aboard*, which became *Gumbo Ya-
Ya*, which then became *Girls! Girls! Girls!* Perhaps the worst series of
titles belonged to *Spinout* because they were mostly meaningless cli-
chés. Those considered included *Jim Dandy, After Midnight, Always
at Midnight, Never Say No,* and *Never Say Yes.* To complicate mat-
ters, its British release title was *California Holiday.*

Favorite Dialogue from Elvis Flicks

Bernice: I'll bet you're a marvelous lover.

Greg (Elvis): I'm representing the United States in the Olympics.

—Live a Little, Love a Little

Myth vs. Fact

Contrary to popular belief, Elvis appeared in more than just teen musicals during the 1960s. He starred in the western *Flaming Star*, the dramas *Wild in the Country* and *Kid Galahad*, and the satire *Follow That Dream*. These films are often pushed aside by biographers who want to paint the 1960s as a decline in Elvis's career or music historians and critics who blame the films for "taming" Elvis. Elvis's image did change after he returned from the army, and his music evolved into a mainstream pop style, but the changes were in keeping with the styles and trends of the early 1960s.

Still, by the mid–1960s, Elvis seemed stuck in a musical comedy rut. Elvis came to despise these films, partly because he never liked the genre to begin with and partly because **he wanted to be a serious actor.** However, there is no proof that Elvis would have been successful as a dramatic actor in the long term.

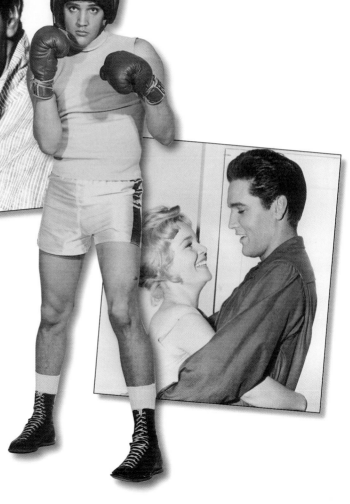

From top left: Flaming Star, Kid Galahad, *and* Wild in the Country

Famed pop artist *Andy Warhol* repeated a film still of Elvis in a series of silk screens produced in the early 1960s. The still was taken from *Flaming Star.* These prints comment on the superficial nature of Hollywood stardom, and the repetition of the image suggests the lack of individual expression inherent in mass-produced art forms, such as the Hollywood movie or the silk screen process. Interestingly, other artists took Warhol's famous silk screen and expanded on it to create new pieces, including Richard Pettibone with *Andy Warhol, Two Elvis, 1964.* and Jerry Kearns with *Earth Angel.*

The use of Elvis imagery in fine art confirms that his impact on culture extends beyond the range of his own art. In life, Elvis blurred the line between black and white cultures with his music; in death, he blurs the line between high and low culture with his image.

More Great Movie Tunes

"Blue Hawaii" from *Blue Hawaii*

"Rock-a-Hula Baby"
from *Blue Hawaii*

"Follow That Dream" from
Follow That Dream

"Return to Sender" from
Girls! Girls! Girls!

"What'd I Say" from
Viva Las Vegas

"Viva Las Vegas" from
Viva Las Vegas

"Little Egypt" from *Roustabout*

"Drums of the Islands"
from *Paradise,
Hawaiian Style*

SpotLight on

Follow That Dream

The title *Follow That Dream* suggests that it is another one of Elvis's romantic musical comedies. While there is music, romance, and comedy, the film differs from his other 1960s films because it was adapted from the satiric novel *Pioneer, Go Home* by Richard Powell. Powell's book is sharper and more complex than the film, but the script by Hollywood veteran Charles Lederer does feature some witty jabs at modern life.

The story follows the Kwimpers, a backwoods family who decide to homestead on a stretch of beach along a Florida highway, much to the chagrin of local officials. Elvis plays Toby Kwimper, the handsome oldest son who, despite being a bit dim-witted, manages to attract the attention of women. The Kwimpers are honest, simple folk who just don't understand the complexities of the modern world, which offers the film the opportunity to poke a bit of fun at everything from psychology to social bureaucracy.

Advertisements for Follow That Dream

Favorite Dialogue from Elvis Flicks

Toby (Elvis): I like girls alright, except when they start to bother me.

Alisha: Young virile man like you, I should think you'd like to be bothered.

Toby: The botherin' part is alright, but I ain't gonna marry no girl and build no house just so I can be bothered regular.

—Follow That Dream

Shooting on actual Florida beaches added a touch of authenticity to *Follow That Dream,* but location filming did give the producers minor headaches. The temperature soared past 100 degrees one week, making it difficult on the cast, crew, and equipment. Elvis had to change his shirt 22 times in one day because he was perspiring so much.

How Great Thou Art
A Break from the Movies

From January 1964 to May 1966, Elvis recorded nothing but movie soundtracks, mostly in Hollywood. Unsatisfied with his life for complex professional and personal reasons, he did not venture into the Nashville studios to cut any album material. When

Jake Hess

he finally decided to record new material, he returned to the studio with new musicians and a new producer, Felton Jarvis.

Felton Jarvis

Elvis went to RCA studios in Nashville in spring 1966 to make a gospel album, *How Great Thou Art*. As a child of the South, he was steeped in gospel music, and he especially liked the four-part harmony style sung by male gospel quartets associated with the shape note singing schools from the early 20th century. Elvis's favorite gospel quartets included the Blackwood Brothers, whom he knew personally, and the Statesmen, whose lead singer was the colorful Jake Hess. Elvis asked Hess and his new group, the Imperials, to join him on this album. *How Great Thou Art* proved to be a milestone in Elvis's career, winning him the first of his three Grammys, this one for Best Sacred Performance.

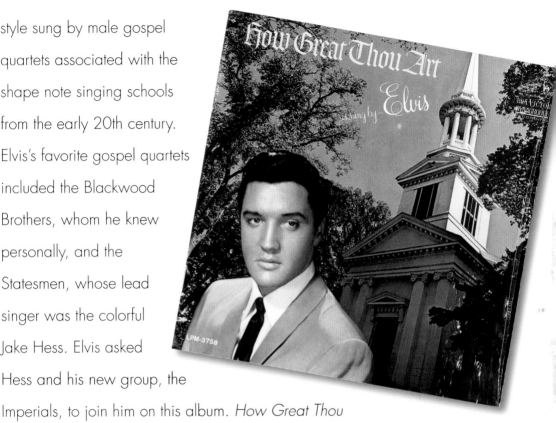

The Worst Movie Tunes

"No Room to Rhumba in a Sports Car"
from *Fun in Acapulco*

"Fort Lauderdale Chamber of Commerce"
from *Girl Happy*

"Do the Clam"
from *Girl Happy*

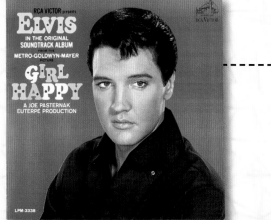

"Barefoot Ballad" from *Kissin' Cousins*

"Yoga Is as Yoga Does" from *Easy Come, Easy Go*

"He's Your Uncle, Not Your Dad" from *Speedway*- - - - - - - -

"Petunia, the Gardener's Daughter" from *Frankie and Johnny*

"Queenie Wahini's Papaya" from *Paradise, Hawaiian Style* - - - - - - - -

Viva Las Vegas

When Elvis returned to Hollywood in July 1963 to begin work on *Viva Las Vegas,* little did he realize he was about to meet his on-screen match. Ann-Margret was a starlet on the rise when she agreed to costar in Elvis's 15th film. A singer-dancer, Ann-Margret injected the film's musical numbers with a vitality and professionalism that had been lacking in Elvis's films for some time. Elvis matched her youthful eagerness with enthusiasm. It surprised no one when the on-screen sparks between Elvis and Ann-Margret ignited a passionate relationship offscreen as well.

Viva Las Vegas was a critical and popular success. It grossed $4.6 million at the box office, making it the 14th-highest grosser of the year. Reviews were generally good. One critic was more perceptive than most when he remarked, "For once everybody in the cast of an Elvis Presley picture isn't overshadowed by the rock 'n' roll hero." Colonel Tom Parker and Elvis's management team preferred that a Presley vehicle showcase only Elvis Presley. After *Viva Las Vegas*, Elvis would never again woo a leading lady with the talent and charisma of Ann-Margret—either on or off the screen.

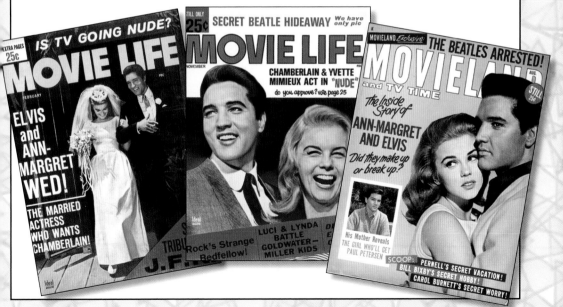

Favorite Dialogue from Elvis Flicks

Rusty (Ann-Margret): I'd like you to check my motor. It whistles.

Lucky (Elvis): I don't blame it.

—Viva Las Vegas

Ann-Margret shared many things in common with Elvis, including the pressure of a show business career. Both enjoyed similar activities, such as riding motorcycles, and she got along well with members of Elvis's entourage. They called her "Rusty Ammo" or "Ann-Margrock."

Dances

David Winters, who choreographed several Elvis films as well as the television series *Hullabaloo*, was asked to invent a dance for *Girl Happy*. Winters came up with the Clam, which was introduced in the song "Do the Clam." Unfortunately, the Clam did not catch on like other 1960s dance crazes such as the Pony, the Monkey, or the Jerk.

The Clam was not the only dance that was spotlighted in an Elvis Presley film. The Forte Four sing "The Climb" in *Viva Las Vegas*, with Elvis, Ann-Margret, and a group of teens performing the dance steps that went with the song. In *Blue Hawaii*, Elvis introduced a dance called Slicin' Sand with a song by the same name, but like the Clam, the dance did not catch on.

From top: The Climb, Slicin' Sand, and the Clam

Norman Taurog was responsible for nine Elvis Presley features—more than any other director. Elvis always favored Taurog, probably because of his kind nature and lack of ego. After particularly difficult scenes, the fatherly director would pass out candy bars to his cast and crew. Taurog was known primarily for lightweight vehicles and comedies, a specialty that dated all the way back to 1919 when his directorial career was launched with a series starring silent comedian Larry Semon. The consummate studio director, Taurog directed many major stars in more than 70 films across six decades. He won an Oscar in 1931 for Skippy, a vehicle for child star Jackie Cooper, and he was nominated again in 1938 for the classic Boys Town. *Taurog died in 1981.*

"I was always **proud of his work,** even if I wasn't proud of the scripts. I always felt that he never reached his peak."

—Norman Taurog

Small Parts for Big Actors

- **Christina Crawford,** Joan Crawford's daughter and author of *Mommie Dearest*, played Monica George in *Wild in the Country*.

Joan O'Brien, Elvis, and a young Kurt Russell

- **Charles Bronson,** a major action star of the 1970s, costarred as Lew Nyack in *Kid Galahad*. Also, a young **Ed Asner,** who played Lou Grant in two highly successful television series, made the most of a small role.

- **Kurt Russell,** who would later play Elvis in a made-for-TV film, appears as a kid who kicks Elvis in the shin in *It Happened at the World's Fair*.

- **Teri Garr,** the girl-next-door in several famous films of the 1980s, can claim the crown for appearing in bit parts in the most Elvis films. Look closely and you can see her as a dancer in *Viva Las Vegas, Roustabout,* and *Clambake,* and as an extra in *Kissin' Cousins* and *Fun in Acapulco.*
- **Richard Kiel,** who played Jaws in the James Bond film *The Spy Who Loved Me,* made a brief appearance as the carnival strong man in *Roustabout.* **Raquel Welch** also showed up, playing a college girl.
- **Dan Haggerty,** who enjoyed fame as the title character in TV's *Grizzly Adams,* played Charlie in *Girl Happy.*
- **Michael Murphy,** one of Woody Allen's key actors during the 1970s and the star of the innovative TV show *Tanner '88,* made his second screen appearance as Morley in *Double Trouble.*
- **Dabney Coleman,** everyone's favorite oily villain in such films as *9 to 5,* played Harrison Wilby in *The Trouble with Girls.*
- **Jane Elliot,** who has played Tracy Quartermaine on *General Hospital* for two decades, got her big break as Sister Barbara Bennett in *Change of Habit.*

A Singing Race-Car Driver, Pilot, or Rodeo Performer

Elvis's characters worked in a variety of colorful and romantic occupations, which was an expected part of his musical comedies. His most frequent occupation was as a performer of some kind, generally a singer, as in *Girl Happy* and *Double Trouble*, but he also played an actor in *Harum Scarum* and the manager of a Chautauqua in *The Trouble with Girls*.

When he wasn't playing a performer, Elvis often played a race-car driver. He was a racer in *Viva Las Vegas*, *Spinout*, and *Speedway*. Other repeated occupations were an airplane pilot in *It Happened at the World's Fair* and *Paradise, Hawaiian Style*, and a rodeo performer in *Tickle Me* and *Stay Away, Joe*. No matter how exotic the occupation (remember the trapeze artist-turned-lifeguard in *Fun in Acapulco*), his characters could always sing!

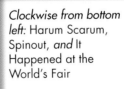

Clockwise from bottom left: Harum Scarum, Spinout, *and* It Happened at the World's Fair

Charro!

With its gritty look, violent antihero, and cynical point of view, *Charro!* was obviously patterned after the grim Italian westerns of the 1960s. Elvis's character, Jess Wade, is costumed similarly to Clint Eastwood's notorious "Man with No Name" from Sergio Leone's Italian westerns. Both wore a scruffy beard and dust-covered western garb, and both kept a well-worn cigar in their mouths. The music in *Charro!* was scored by Hugh Montenegro, who was responsible for the memorable score of *The Good, the Bad, and the Ugly*. Unfortunately, director Charles Marquis Warren was no match for

Charro! *was a departure from Elvis's usual musical comedies.*

Sergio Leone, and *Charro!* suffers from poor production values.

At the time, much was made about the absence of songs in the film, as though that fact proved *Charro!* was

Ads for *Charro!* emphasized the difference from Elvis's other films.

a serious effort. Advertisements for the film declared that *Charro!* featured "a different kind of role . . . a different kind of man." Elvis granted more interviews and generated more publicity for *Charro!* than he had for any film in a long time. One interview quoted him as saying "*Charro!* is the first movie I ever made without singing a song. I play a gunfighter, and I just couldn't see a singing gunfighter." Eventually, Elvis did agree to sing the title tune, but there are no songs within the body of the film.

Elvis's Best Costars

Elvis worked with some of the best actors in Hollywood, past and present. Some were movie stars, some starlets, some character actors, and some veterans from another era, but all added depth and professionalism to the performances in the films.

Richard Egan in *Love Me Tender*

Walter Matthau and Carolyn Jones in *King Creole*

Juliet Prowse in *G. I. Blues*

Dolores Del Rio and John McIntire in *Flaming Star*

Angela Lansbury in *Blue Hawaii*

Gig Young in *Kid Galahad*

Tuesday Weld in
Wild in the Country - - - - - - - - - -

Arthur O'Connell in
Follow That Dream

Ann-Margret in *Viva Las Vegas*

Barbara Stanwyck in *Roustabout*

Sue Ane Langdon in
Frankie and Johnny

Joan Blondell in *Stay Away, Joe*

Mary Tyler Moore and
Jane Elliot in *Change of Habit* - - - - - -

Bubbly **Shelley Fabares** *was supposedly Elvis's favorite costar. She appeared in* Girl Happy, Clambake, *and* Spinout. *A child actress, Fabares got her start on the TV sitcom* The Donna Reed Show. *She eventually returned to a career on the small screen.*

No stranger to the pop music scene, Shelley Fabares had recorded "Johnny Angel," a number-one hit in 1962.

What Might Have Been

During the years that Elvis was an actor in Hollywood, he had several opportunities to star in films that were not "Presley travelogues," but these opportunities fell through. Often, the Colonel refused to agree to a film that did not follow the formula or did not showcase Elvis to his

A Star Is Born

best advantage. He turned down the 1956 rock 'n' roll spoof *The Girl Can't Help It,* because the money wasn't good enough and because Elvis would have had to share the screen with other notable rock 'n' roll acts. In the 1970s, Barbra Streisand was rumored to have wanted Elvis for her remake of *A Star Is Born,* but supposedly the Colonel turned her down. Kris Kristofferson played the role. Other roles that Elvis turned down included Hank Williams in *Your Cheatin' Heart* (George Hamilton played Williams) and the singing cowboy in *The Fastest Guitar in the West* (Roy Orbison got the part). Rumors persist that Elvis could have appeared in *Thunder Road, The*

Thunder Road

Way to the Gold, and *The Defiant Ones,* but these rumors may have been born of bitterness over Elvis's lost potential as an actor. Other factors prevented Elvis from appearing in certain films, including the timing of projects and failed deals. Elvis was once set to play a James Bond–like superspy in a comedy adventure called *That Jack Valentine,* but the film was never produced. Other projects that fell through included a proposed musical starring Elvis opposite a classical artist and a comedy teaming Elvis with French legend Brigitte Bardot.

Time Out for Marriage

Priscilla Beaulieu had been living at Graceland for several years, maintaining a low profile to keep the press away, but on May 1, 1967, Elvis brought his princess out of hiding. He and Priscilla were married at the Aladdin Hotel in Las Vegas. The double-ring ceremony lasted only eight minutes and took place in a suite owned by one of the Colonel's friends. Only a few of Elvis's buddies were allowed to witness the actual event, causing some dissension in the ranks of the Memphis Mafia. Joe Esposito and Marty Lacker served as best men, and Priscilla's sister, Michelle, was the maid of honor. After the ceremony, there was a breakfast reception for 100 at the Aladdin, which was an event held primarily for the press. Elvis and Priscilla honeymooned in Palm Springs, California. On February 1, 1968, nine months to the day after Elvis and Priscilla were married, Lisa Marie Presley was born.

Elvis and Priscilla leave the hospital with their newborn daughter, Lisa Marie.

The Films of Elvis Presley

King Creole (1958)

G. I. Blues (1960)

Flaming Star (1960)

Wild in the Country (1961)

Blue Hawaii (1961)

Follow That Dream (1962)

Kid Galahad (1962)

Girls! Girls! Girls! (1962)

It Happened at the World's Fair (1963)

Fun in Acapulco (1963)

Kissin' Cousins (1964)

Viva Las Vegas (1964)

Love Me Tender (1956)

Loving You (1957)

Jailhouse Rock (1957)

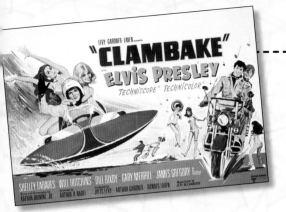

Roustabout (1964)

Girl Happy (1965)

Tickle Me (1965)

Harum Scarum (1965)

Frankie and Johnny (1966)

Paradise, Hawaiian Style (1966)

Spinout (1966)

Easy Come, Easy Go (1967)

Double Trouble (1967)

Clambake (1967)

Stay Away, Joe (1968)

Speedway (1968)

Live a Little, Love a Little (1968)

Charro! (1969)

The Trouble with Girls (1969)

Change of Habit (1969)

Elvis: That's the Way It Is (1970)

Elvis on Tour (1972)

CHAPTER 4

One Night with You:
Concert King

"*Presley remains a true American artist*—one of the greatest in American popular music, a singer of native brilliance and a performer of magnetic dimensions."

—*Jim Millar*, Rolling Stone

Energized by the positive reception for *The '68 Comeback Special*, Elvis *returned to the stage to perform* before a live audience. He tested the waters with an engagement at the International Hotel in Las Vegas in 1969, a critically acclaimed performance attended by the biggest celebrities of the day. Shortly thereafter, he hit the road again to tour the country. For the rest of his life, Elvis alternated between Vegas engagements and extensive touring.

In his stage performances, Elvis was not content to sing the songs that made him famous during the 1950s. He did perform a medley of his old rockabilly classics in an updated arrangement, but his act was organized around contemporary tunes. Elvis had eclectic taste in music, a characteristic that is generally underappreciated and rarely acknowledged. During the concert era, he featured country, pop, rhythm-and-blues, and rock, moving easily from one genre to another without missing a beat. Impossible to classify as a singer and influenced only by the quality of a song, Elvis Presley refused to be bound by a single genre—or by musical limits of any kind.

Left: **Loving You**
Above: **Stay Away, Joe**
Right: **King Creole**

With this witty quip, Elvis effectively summed up his opinion on his film career and explained his renewed focus on music:

"I get tired of playing a guy who gets into a fight, then starts singing to the guy he's just beat up."

—**Newsweek,**
August 11, 1969

The '68 Comeback Special

In early 1968, Colonel Tom Parker closed a deal for Elvis to appear in his own television special for NBC. It was taped in late June and aired on December 3. The Colonel's vision of the special had Elvis walking in front of a Christmas tree, singing favorite familiar carols, and then wishing everyone a happy holiday. However, Steve Binder, the producer of the special, had a different vision. He hoped to capture what he felt was Elvis's genius—the adaptation of rhythm-and-blues to the tastes of mainstream audiences. He wanted to prove that Elvis was not a relic of rock 'n' roll's past.

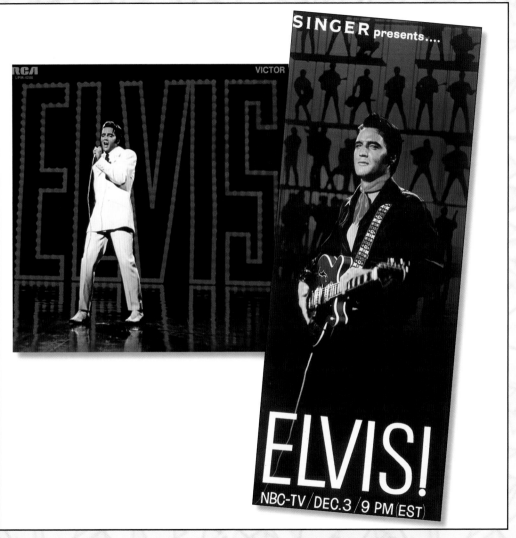

The '68 Comeback Special

- The original name of *The '68 Comeback Special* was simply *Elvis*. It aired on December 3, 1968.

- The special was sponsored by Singer Sewing Machines, and some of the promotional material refers to it as *Singer Presents Elvis*.

- Elvis wore a gold lamé jacket while performing "Trouble," which echoed his famous lamé suit from 1958 without exactly duplicating it. The approach was meant to remind viewers of the pre-movie Elvis without making him a carbon copy of the past.

- In the concert segment, Elvis and four musicians sat on a small stage and reminisced about the past while performing updated versions of Elvis hits. Two of those musicians were Scotty Moore and D. J. Fontana, two-thirds of the Blue Moon Boys.

- The special received a 32 rating and a 42 share, making it the highest-rated program the week that it was broadcast.

The '68 Comeback Special closed with the moving spiritual *"If I Can Dream."* The song was written at the last minute at the request of the show's producer, Steve Binder. The musical director of *The '68 Comeback Special*, W. Earl Brown, wrote the song as a response to the assassinations of Robert Kennedy and Martin Luther King Jr. It was intended as a statement of hope for the future. Elvis loved "If I Can Dream," and he gave it all he had.

The instrumental track was recorded on June 20 or 21, 1968. Elvis sang the song in front of the orchestra's string section while the instrumental part was being recorded. Though his vocals were not to be used on the final version, he sang with all the passion the song inspired, even dropping down on his knee at one point. The effect left the string section with their mouths agape. Later, Elvis rerecorded the vocals in a darkened studio, and once again, he performed the song rather than merely recording it.

The Black Leather Suit

For one segment of *The '68 Comeback Special*, Scotty Moore and D. J. Fontana reunited with Elvis onstage for an informal jam session. Elvis reminisced about his early career and belted out several of his famous hits with fresh and exciting new arrangements. The black leather ensemble that he wore in this segment is the most famous costume from *The '68 Comeback Special*. Designed by Bill Belew, the costume has become iconic. Indeed, it is synonymous with Elvis's creative comeback in the

late 1960s. Like the new arrangements of his songs, the black leather outfit recalled the past but did not duplicate it. The comeback special aired at the close of 1968, when flower children held love-ins and wore paisley and posies. In the midst of the Age of Aquarius, a drop-dead handsome Elvis Presley strolled onstage in black leather, a guitar cocked on his hip, and reminded us that rock 'n' roll was not about peace and harmony—it was really about sexuality and rebellion.

"[Clothes] say things about you that you can't, sometimes."

—Elvis, reprinted in
The World According to Elvis,
1992

"There is something special about **watching a man who has lost himself find his way back home.** He sang with the kind of power people no longer associate with rock 'n' roll singers. He moved his body with a lack of pretension and effort that must have made Jim Morrison green with envy. And while most of the songs were ten or twelve years old, he performed them as freshly as though they were written yesterday."

—*Rock critic Jon Landau on* **The '68 Comeback Special**

Inspired and invigorated by the success of his television special, Elvis walked through the door of tiny American Sound Studios in Memphis in January 1969 to make quality music that would garner him hit records. Elvis had not recorded in his hometown since he left Sun in 1955, but the musical atmosphere at RCA's Nashville studios had become stale. His friends and associates encouraged him to record at American Sound because Nashville would yield nothing for him at this time.

American Sound Studios, a small studio in a run-down neighborhood, was operated by Chips Moman. With Moman as producer, Elvis worked hard to record his first significant mainstream album in years. In retrospect, *From Elvis in Memphis* may be his most important album because it brought his recording career back from soundtrack purgatory and set a creative standard for the next few years. No longer the crooning movie star, Elvis had returned to the music scene to reclaim his crown as the King of Rock 'n' Roll.

The house band at American Sound Studios included musicians who were steeped in all forms of Southern music. Both black and white artists recorded at American Sound, and the house band was generally the same no matter who recorded

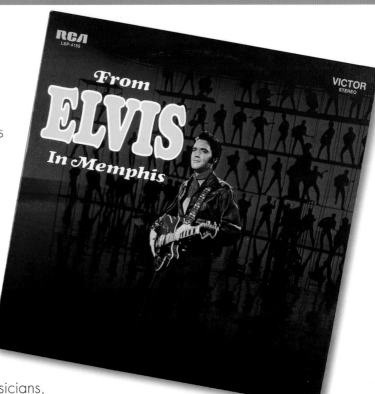

there. Many of these musicians, including guitarist Reggie Young, bassist Tommy Cogbill, and pianist Bobby Wood, grew up listening to Elvis's music. No other fitting group of musicians could have backed Elvis on his return to Memphis.

A Return to the Stage
Las Vegas, July 31, 1969

After the benefit for the USS *Arizona* at Bloch Arena at Pearl Harbor in 1961, Elvis did not perform before a live audience for more than eight years. Invigorated by his 1968 television special and his first major album in years, *From Elvis in Memphis*, he accepted an offer to perform in the new 2,000-seat showroom of the International Hotel in Las Vegas (later the Hilton). Barbra Streisand had opened the room the previous month, and Elvis attended her closing night. Elvis had rehearsed for a month with his new band, and despite a few glitches, the audience of celebrities and reporters responded to his opening night with a standing ovation. In his new act, Elvis performed a medley of his greatest hits but also included new material from his recent recording sessions in Memphis. Reviews of his nearly sold-out engagement were positive. Total attendance exceeded 101,509, which was a Vegas record, as was the $1,522,635 box-office take.

Myth vs. Fact

Colonel Tom Parker is often painted as the **villain in the Elvis Presley legend.** With his oddball deals, gruff tone, carnival huckster past, and lack of foresight in some aspects of Elvis's career, it is easy for many biographers to present him as a ruthless, cold-hearted manager who did not have Elvis's best interests at heart.

Priscilla Beaulieu Presley, in her account of her life with Elvis, reveals a touching story about Colonel Parker. Backstage at the International Hotel, after Elvis's triumphant return to concert performing, many celebrities and well wishers were on hand to congratulate the King. At this moment of great personal and professional triumph for his one and only client, Parker pushed his way backstage. Everyone could see that tears were welling up in his eyes. Where was "his boy," he wanted to know. As Elvis emerged from his dressing

room, the two men embraced, too overcome with emotion to speak. Over the years, there have been many stories about Parker that have illustrated his greed and his mistakes, but perhaps no story reveals the complexity of the relationship between Elvis and the Colonel better than this one.

The Concert Band

A consequence of Elvis's new direction in the 1970s was a change in the core group of musicians who recorded and toured with him. Chief among these musicians was lead guitarist James Burton, who had worked with Ricky Nelson. An accomplished and respected lead guitar player, Burton later worked with Gram Parsons and Emmylou Harris. Other band members included several Hollywood session musicians who had occasionally contributed to Elvis's movie soundtracks: bassist Jerry Scheff, who had worked with the Doors; pianist Larry Muhoberac; and drummer Ronnie Tutt. Elvis's new sound was large-scale, almost operatic. In addition to musicians, he used a male gospel quartet and a female backup group in his recording sessions and on the road. At first the Imperials gospel quartet, with the legendary Jake Hess, backed Elvis vocally, but later J. D. Sumner and the Stamps Quartet took over that role. The Sweet Inspirations fulfilled the duties as female backup voices, and Kathy Westmoreland supplied an additional soprano voice.

Guitarist James Burton (left) and drummer Ronnie Tutt (below) toured with Elvis in the 1970s.

Elvis and Christmas

Christmas was Elvis's favorite time of year, which is reflected by the many holiday singles and albums that he recorded over the years.

October 1971

November 1957

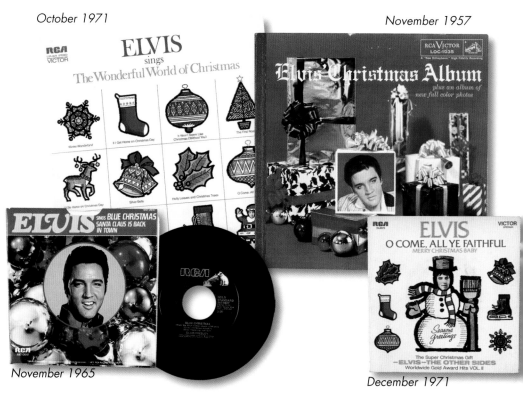

November 1965

December 1971

Throughout his life, Elvis loved celebrating the Christmas season with family and friends. In this 1957 photo, Elvis shows off a few of his holiday gifts.

Elvis's last number-one single, *"Suspicious Minds,"* offers an example of the large-scale sound that defined his later style. At four minutes and 22 seconds, it is his longest number-one song, and in his Las Vegas shows, he stretched it into a powerhouse, showstopping piece that ran eight minutes. Elvis had introduced the song in Vegas on July 26, 1969, during his first live performance at the International Hotel. It was not released as a single until the following September. The song entered *Billboard*'s Hot 100 chart, peaking at the number-one position seven weeks later.

The song was originally recorded at American Sound Studios in Memphis on January 23, 1969, though it was held for release until a later date. "Suspicious Minds" featured backing vocals by Jeannie Green and Ronnie Milsap, a singer-songwriter who later became a prominent country-western star. To help achieve the large-scale sound, Elvis's Las Vegas band was overdubbed at a Vegas recording studio in August. Also, the end of the song was spliced on for a second time. This overdubbing and remixing was supervised by Elvis's producer, Felton Jarvis.

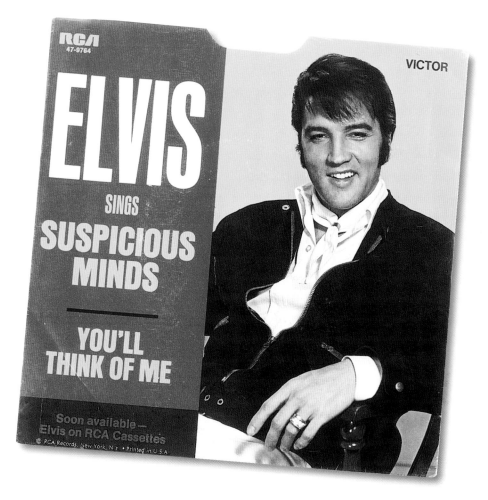

Almost as Famous as Elvis

During his lifetime, Elvis respected the talent of many other performers and celebrities, even if their styles or arenas of performance differed from his.

"One night I went into the casino after the show, and I saw [Bobby Darin] standing there with Elvis Presley.... both of them were beautiful, polite, talented kids. I thought I'd make them laugh. So...I whispered, 'I see you fellows are alone. If you need any help meeting girls, don't be embarrassed to ask me.' Presley thought I was serious. 'Thank you, Mr. Burns,' he said. Toughest audience I ever worked to."

—*George Burns, reprinted in*
Elvis! The Last Word, *1991*

Elvis and Bobby Darin

Tom Jones, Priscilla, and Elvis

Elvis and Liberace

Muhammad Ali and Elvis

Best Reinvented Songs
by Elvis

"That's All Right" was written and recorded by Arthur "Big Boy" Crudup as a country blues tune in 1947 and reworked by Elvis in 1955. Elvis's fast-paced, rockabilly interpretation became his first single.

Elvis recorded two versions of the Dave Bartholomew–Pearl King blues tune "One Night of Sin," which had been a hit for Smiley Lewis in 1956. On January 24, 1957, he recorded the Smiley Lewis version, and a month later he rerecorded the song as "One Night," using cleaned-up lyrics. In Lewis's risqué original, the singer is praying for "One night of sin," while in Elvis's more hopeful rendition of the song, he is yearning for "One night with you . . . ."

Tin Pan Alley song-writers Lou Handman and Roy Turk composed "Are You Lonesome Tonight?" ("To-night" on the original record sleeve) in 1926, and it was originally recorded by Al Jolson the following year. Supposedly the only song Colonel Tom Parker ever urged Elvis to record, "Are You Lonesome Tonight?" was released by Elvis in 1960 and was nominated for three Grammys.

Elvis sang James Taylor's 1970 composition "Steamroller Blues" in concert during the early 1970s, but his gritty rendition during the *Aloha from Hawaii* television special stopped the show. The version from the special was released as a single in April 1973.

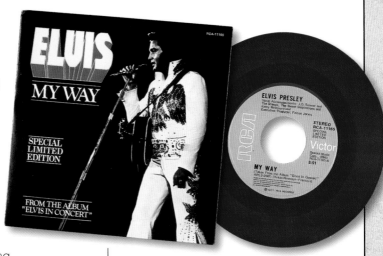

"My Way," an anthem of independence and individuality, was written by Paul Anka for Frank Sinatra and originally recorded by Sinatra in 1969. Elvis sang "My Way" on the *Aloha from Hawaii* television special and in concert during the 1970s. A recording of this song by Elvis was released shortly after he died, making it almost a biographical statement.

After Elvis's discharge from the army, the entertainment press discovered that he was accompanied by an entourage of about 20 friends and associates wherever he traveled. The press dubbed them the "Memphis Mafia" or the "Tennessee Mafia," just as they had called Frank Sinatra's gang of celebrity friends the "Rat Pack." However, the differences between the Rat Pack and the Memphis Mafia became apparent as Elvis's career continued, and the press never quite seemed to grasp the gang's relationship to Elvis.

Most of the members of the Memphis Mafia were hometown boys from Memphis, family members, or friends Elvis had met in the army. Many of them actually lived with Elvis. They accompanied Elvis to the set, drove him to and from the studio, and worked as bodyguards to keep fans and the press away. The closeness of this group of friends and employees made Elvis feel at home in Hollywood or on the road, but it also isolated him from industry insiders and fellow entertainers who could have been a positive influence on him.

Elvis was infatuated with law enforcement most of his life. Here, Elvis and his entourage show off honorary deputy badges from Shelby County, Tennessee.

The Astrodome
Houston, Texas
February 27–March 1, 1970

Elvis's Las Vegas engagements in August 1969 and February 1970 represented his return to live performances, but his three-day gig at the Houston Astrodome launched his return to touring. The show was part of the Texas Livestock Show and Rodeo, and Elvis held two press conferences in conjunction with his engagement. At one, he acknowledged the importance of country music to his career and told reporters he was happy that it had increased in popularity. Though significant in terms of his career, the Astrodome engagement was not his best work, mainly due to problems with the equipment and microphones. Local reviews were positive, but they noted that the Astrodome was not the best place to see any type of musical concert. It was an enormous arena that even Elvis found somewhat intimidating. Still, his six shows drew 207,494 people.

From 1963 through 1980, *RCA Records* printed *pocket calendars* with Elvis's picture on one side and a 12-month calendar on the other. To promote goodwill, as well as Elvis's singles and albums, RCA issued the calendars to fan clubs and to record stores as giveaways for their customers. Versions of the calendars were printed for foreign markets as well, including Germany and Japan. The promotion proved to be a popular one, particularly after Elvis died. The rarest and most valuable calendar is

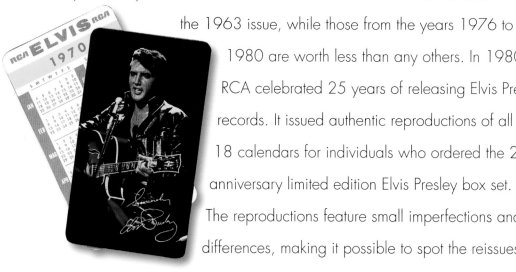

the 1963 issue, while those from the years 1976 to 1980 are worth less than any others. In 1980, RCA celebrated 25 years of releasing Elvis Presley records. It issued authentic reproductions of all 18 calendars for individuals who ordered the 25th anniversary limited edition Elvis Presley box set. The reproductions feature small imperfections and differences, making it possible to spot the reissues.

Outstanding Young Man of America

On January 16, 1971, Elvis Presley was named one of the Ten Outstanding Young Men of America by the Junior Chamber of Commerce (Jaycees), a nationally based community group devoted to civic duty. Each year, the Jaycees nominate young men, usually under the age of 30, who are praiseworthy in their fields. A panel of distinguished judges makes the final selection of ten. The judges, including former President Lyndon B. Johnson, chose Elvis not only because he was the greatest entertainer of his time but also because of his many acts of philanthropy and charity. Visitors who see the Jaycees award at Graceland cannot help but notice the scuff and scratch marks. Elvis carried the statue with him on every tour and trip until he died.

With Priscilla by his side, Elvis is honored by the Jaycees.

"I learned very early in life that without a song, the day would never end; **without a song, a man ain't got a friend;** without a song, the road would never bend—without a song. So I keep singing a song . . . ."

—Elvis, on accepting the Jaycees' Outstanding Young Man of America Award

Elvis Drops in on a President

In December 1970, Elvis made a spontaneous decision to travel to Washington, D.C., to visit Deputy U.S. Narcotics Director John Finlator. Although Elvis said that he was going to volunteer his help in the antidrug campaign, he was actually hoping to obtain a federal narcotics badge to add to his collection. Finlator turned down Elvis's request for a badge, but Elvis decided to go over Finlator's head. With a couple of members of the Memphis Mafia, Elvis called on President Richard Nixon at the White House. The charismatic Presley was able to talk Nixon into giving him an authentic narcotics agent's badge in a matter of minutes.

On later trips, Elvis visited FBI headquarters to offer his assistance in fighting the war on drugs. While it's not surprising that Elvis visited law-enforcement agencies, the fact that he could get in to see the president on a few hours' notice is extraordinary testimony to Elvis's amazing popularity and power. Other entertainers have been honored by invitations to perform at the White House, but the King simply dropped in to get something he wanted.

Elvis's 32nd film, *Elvis: That's the Way It Is,* was not a narrative feature but a documentary showcasing his 1970 summer appearance at the International Hotel in Las Vegas. Elvis began rehearsals July 5 at the MGM studios in Hollywood, where he worked on his material for about a month. The show opened August 10. The MGM cameras not only recorded the rehearsals but also opening night, several performances throughout the engagement, and one show at Veterans Memorial Coliseum in Phoenix, Arizona. The film is structured so that the rehearsals and other scenes of preparation build to an extended climax of Elvis onstage. Performing in a simple white jumpsuit accented with fringe instead of rhinestones and gems, Elvis is captured at the pinnacle of his career.

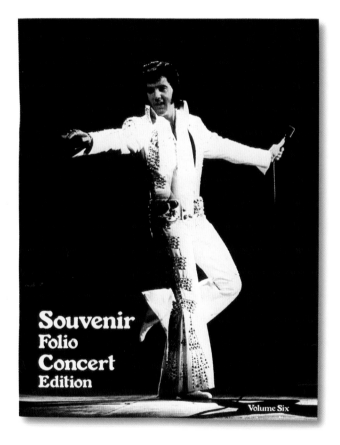

Souvenir
Folio
Concert
Edition

Volume Six

"**A live concert** to me **is exciting** because of all the electricity that is generated in the crowd and on stage. It's my favorite part of the business—live concerts."

—*Elvis, 1973*

The highlight of Elvis's studio sessions during March 1972 was the recording of "Burning Love." By this point, Elvis and his band were masters of this type of large-scale, fast-rocking number, and his interpretation of the song typifies his 1970s sound.

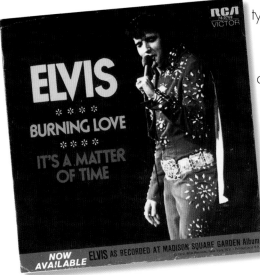

Dennis Linde composed "Burning Love" and played guitar on the recording. It was Linde who dubbed in the raucous guitar licks on the bridges of the song. He had occasionally served as a bass guitarist in Elvis's recording band during the 1970s.

"Burning Love" became a worldwide hit for Elvis in 1972, and it quickly charted on *Billboard's* Hot 100. Peaking at number two, it just missed becoming a number-one record. Chuck Berry's "My Ding-a-Ling" kept "Burning Love" from hitting the top of the charts. The record was certified gold by the RIAA in October 1972, and it was certified platinum in March 1992.

"Burning Love" Jumpsuit

Elvis wore a bright red jumpsuit onstage during his fall tour in 1972. The costume quickly became a fan favorite and one of his most famous stage costumes. Fans began referring to it as the "Burning Love" jumpsuit, perhaps because of its color. Also, the song "Burning Love" was included in set lists for his tour that year. Confusion exists about the "Burning Love" jumpsuit because the white costume and cape worn onstage at the Madison Square Garden engagement in June 1972 had once been given the same name. Elvis appears in the white suit on the cover of the album *Burning Love and Hits from His Movies, Volume 2,* which is why that costume had originally been christened "Burning Love." However, the title seemed better suited to the red stage costume, and over time, the red suit usurped the cherished nickname. Elvis donated the red suit to the National Cerebral Palsy Telethon in 1972. In October 1995, the suit was sold at a Las Vegas auction for a record $107,000.

Elvis performs in the "Burning Love" jumpsuit.

The International became the *Las Vegas Hilton* after Barron Hilton purchased it in 1971. Elvis performed at the hotel from 1969 to 1976. His return to live performances occurred in August 1969 when the hotel was still called the International, and this engagement set a Las Vegas record of 101,509 paying customers who generated a gross take of $1.5 million. Suites 446 and 447 of the Hilton were always reserved for Colonel Parker, who was no stranger to the hotel's casino.

Despite the makeover that the city of Las Vegas has undergone since the 1970s, the Hilton has survived. A large statue of Elvis is located inside the casino entrance near the main showroom. Dedicated in 1978, the 400-pound statue is made of bronze. In a nearby glass case is one of Elvis's guitars and next to it is one of his jumpsuits.

OFFICIAL REUNION — SUMMER FESTIVAL

ALWAYS **ELVIS**

LAS VEGAS HILTON

HILTON PAVILION

$15.00
INCLUDING TAX

SEPT. 8, 1978
8:00 P.M.
NO REFUNDS

GENERAL ADMISSION

002083

Madison Square Garden
June 9–11, 1972

Elvis Presley made entertainment history with his four-show engagement at Madison Square Garden. He was the first performer to sell out all of his shows in advance, grossing about $730,000. A total of 80,000 people attended his performances, including John Lennon, David Bowie, Bob Dylan, and George Harrison. During the engagement, Elvis wore sequined jumpsuits and gold-lined capes, which, by 1972, were typical for his concert performances. The Sweet Inspirations, J. D. Sumner and the Stamps Quartet, and Elvis's touring band backed him. The act included a medley of his classic hits, during which he engaged in some self-parody to the delight of the audience. He also performed new material, including the very Southern "An American Trilogy," a song that mystified the New York critics. Remarkably, the engagement marked the first time Elvis had ever given a live concert in New York City.

Jerry Weintraub in Association with RCA Records Tours Presents

ELVIS

JUNE 9-10 AT

madison square garden
Pennsylvania Plaza, 7th Ave., 31st to 33rd Sts.

DON'T MISS IT

FRIDAY NIGHT	SATURDAY MATINEE	SATURDAY NIGHT
June 9-8:30 P.M.	**June 10-2:30 P.M.** Prices:	**June 10-8:30 P.M.** Prices:
$10, $7.50, $5. Tax incl.	**$10, $7.50, $5.** Tax incl.	**$10, $7.50, $5.** Tax incl.

Tickets on sale Monday, May 8th, at Madison Square Garden
For additional information, call (212) 564-4400. Tickets also available at Ticketron outlets
in these cities: New York (212) 644-4400, Boston (617) 655-5440, Philadelphia (215) LO 3-9008,
Pittsburgh (412) 922-5300, Washington, D.C. (202) 659-2601.

NO MAIL ORDERS ACCEPTED.
Hear Elvis on RCA Records and Tapes.

"*Elvis*...materialized in a white suit of lights, shining with golden appliques, the shirt front slashed to show his chest. Around his shoulders was a cape lined in a cloth of gold, its collar faced with scarlet. It was anything you wanted to call it, *gaudy, vulgar— magnificent.*

—*The New York Times,
June 10, 1972,
Madison Square Garden
opening night*

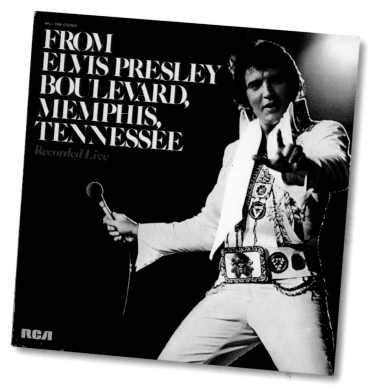

"Ask anyone. If it hadn't been for Elvis, I don't know where popular music would be. **He was the one that started it all off,** and he was definitely the start of it for me."

—Elton John

JUST the Facts

Elvis as Recorded at Madison Square Garden

- RCA recorded all four concerts from Elvis's famous engagement at Madison Square Garden in June 1972.

- The performance from June 10 was used for this album.

- Eager to take advantage of the good press for this series of concerts, which marked the first time Elvis ever played a live engagement in New York City, RCA had the album produced, the records pressed, and the product in stores less than two weeks later.

- The album was certified gold by the RIAA on August 4, 1972.

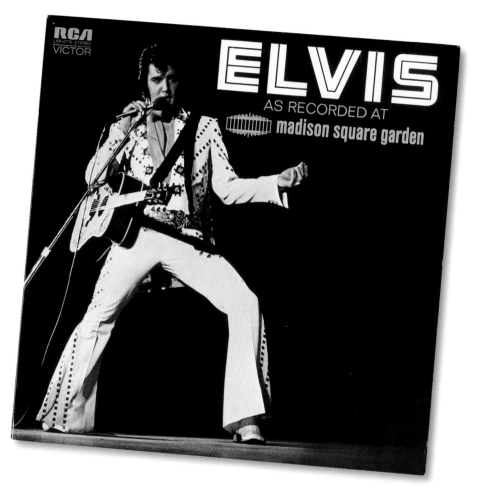

Elvis on Tour

The second documentary to capture Elvis in performance focused on his road show. *Elvis on Tour* followed the singer's 15-city tour in the spring of 1972. The tour started in Buffalo, New York, and came to a rousing conclusion in Albuquerque, New Mexico. Much of the tour centered on the South, where Elvis's popularity peaked in the 1970s.

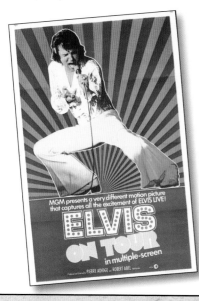

In addition to the footage of Elvis in concert, the film attempted to reveal the real Elvis Presley backstage and off-guard. A camera followed the singer and his entourage, while Elvis was asked to comment on such topics as his music and childhood. According to filmmakers Pierre Adidge and Robert Abel in the press kit for the film, ". . . after we filmed [Elvis] on tour and were allowed to shoot and record in places he had never allowed cameras in the past, we finally asked if he would mind talking about himself. He thought awhile and finally agreed." Despite a few humorous candid moments, however, these interviews did not reveal the real Elvis but only added to the myth that surrounded him.

Originally arranged and recorded by country singer Mickey New-
bury, *"An American Trilogy"* is a medley of
"Dixie," "The Battle Hymn of the Republic," and "All My Trials." The
integration of two Civil War songs (one a Southern anthem, the
other a Northern anthem) with a traditional spiritual suggests the
curiously Southern tradition of blending diverse cultural elements.

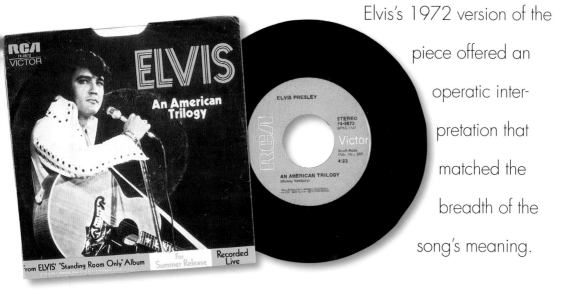

Elvis's 1972 version of the
piece offered an
operatic inter-
pretation that
matched the
breadth of the
song's meaning.

In 1968, country singer Marty Robbins wrote *"You Gave Me a Mountain,"* a wrenching ballad about life's hardships. Though pop star Frankie Laine was the first to release it, Elvis began singing the song in concert during the early 1970s and released it in 1973. Elvis's interpretation is generally considered autobiographical in that it paralleled his breakup with Priscilla Presley.

Elvis's Favorite Snack
Peanut Butter and Banana Sandwich

- 3 tablespoons peanut butter
- 2 slices of light bread
- 1 banana, mashed
- 2 tablespoons margarine, melted

Mix soft peanut butter and mashed banana together. Toast bread lightly. Spread peanut butter and mashed banana on toast. Place into melted margarine in skillet; brown on both sides.

"The image is one thing and the human being is another... *it's very hard to live up to an image.*"

—*Elvis Presley, press conference for Madison Square Garden show, June 1972*

Aloha Elvis

One of Elvis's favorite locations was Hawaii, and the state loomed large in his career. He first visited the islands in November 1957 when he was on tour.

On March 25, 1961, he gave a benefit concert for the USS *Arizona* Memorial Fund, his last public performance until 1969. It was also the last time he wore his gold lamé jacket. The concert took place at Honolulu's Bloch Arena before 4,000 wild fans. The Colonel purchased 50 of the special $100 concert tickets and donated them to hospital patients. Elvis himself donated $5,000 to the Memorial Fund.

On January 14, 1973, Elvis performed before 6,000 people at Honolulu's International Convention Center. The concert became the first to be telecast worldwide. More than 1 billion people in 40 countries saw Elvis's concert, dubbed *Aloha from Hawaii*, which was aired on the mainland on April 4. The concert was a benefit for the Kui Lee Cancer Fund.

Elvis: Aloha from Hawaii was beamed by the Intelsat IV satellite to countries all over the world on January 14, 1973. Broadcast at 12:30 A.M. Hawaii time, the special was seen in Australia, New Zealand, the Philippine Islands, Japan, and other countries in Asia. Even parts of Communist China supposedly tuned in. The next day, the show was rebroadcast to 28 European countries. The special consisted of a concert performance by Elvis in front of a live audience at the Honolulu International Convention Center. After the audience left the arena, Elvis was filmed singing five more songs, which

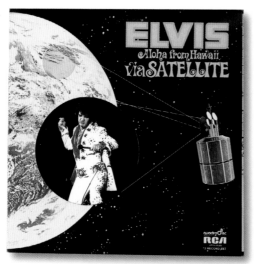

were to be included in the U.S. edition of the concert. NBC's broadcast of the show on April 4 included only four of the additional songs, however. The U.S. broadcast of the special was watched by 51 percent of the television viewing audience—more people than those who watched the first walk on the moon.

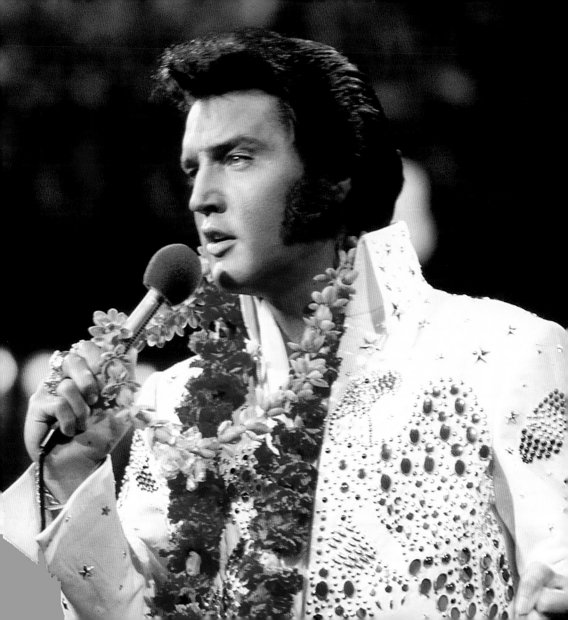

Aloha from Hawaii Jumpsuit

Elvis wanted a costume that signified America for *Aloha from Hawaii*, so designer Bill Belew produced a white jumpsuit with an American eagle patterned in red, gold, and blue gems. The costume's spectacular calf-length cape proved to be too cumbersome during rehearsals, so Elvis ordered a hip-length cape to replace it. A belt decorated with gold American eagles accented the ensemble. During the show, Elvis threw the belt and the cape into the cheering crowd. Elvis ordered a second cape and belt for the jumpsuit and wore the outfit in later performances. The original belt has never surfaced, and the original cape is now in the hands of a private collector. By the end of 1974, Elvis stopped wearing capes onstage. Not only were they heavy and uncomfortable, but members of the audience tended to grab the edges of them while he was performing, resulting in some near accidents.

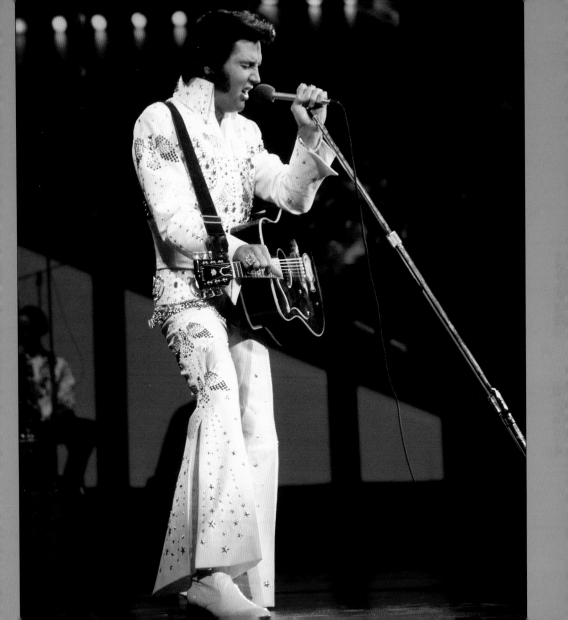

Grammy Awards

Despite his immeasurable impact on 20th-century popular music, Elvis won only three Grammy Awards during his lifetime. The Grammy, the most prestigious award in the music industry, was particularly coveted during Elvis's lifetime because there were far fewer music awards then. In 1967, Elvis won a Grammy for Best Sacred Performance for the album *How Great Thou Art*. Five years later, he won for Best Inspirational Performance for *He Touched Me*. In 1974, he won Best Inspirational Performance for the song "How Great Thou Art" from the album *Elvis Recorded Live on Stage in Memphis*. Because gospel music played such an important role in Elvis's life, he was especially gratified that he won for his inspirational recordings. In addition to his three awards, Elvis was nominated for Grammys ten times during his career. Also, the cover of *For LP Fans Only* was nominated for Best Album Cover in 1959.

"Since I was two years old, all I knew was gospel music. That music became such a part of my life it was *as natural as dancing.* A way to escape from the problems, and my way of release."

—Elvis, reprinted in **Elvis in His Own Words**, *1977*

Master of the Jumpsuit

Bill Belew was the tailor who designed Elvis's concert costumes, beginning in 1968 when he created the black leather suit for *The '68 Comeback Special*. Though most associate the white jumpsuit with this phase of Elvis's career, there was quite a variety to Elvis's outfits. Some costumes were not jumpsuits at all, such as the black mohair suit Elvis wore at the International in 1969. The jumpsuits themselves came in a variety of colors and designs.

*American Eagle
1974*

Black Phoenix 1975

Black Conquistador 1972

Blue Rainbow 1974

The Peacock 1974

Green Cisco
Kid 1971

Tiffany 1972

Indian Feather
1975

CHAPTER 5

Burning Love:
Fan Phenomenon

"This boy had everything. He had **the looks, the moves, the manager, and the talent.** And he didn't look like Mr. Ed like a lot of the rest of us did. In the way he looked, way he talked, way he acted—he really was different."

—*Carl Perkins*

FROM THE DAY ELVIS PRESLEY DIED on August 16, 1977, the fans refused to let his legacy or his talent be forgotten. Despite the rumors that belittled his image and the real-life revelations that shocked the public, Elvis's fans remain loyal—even in the face of a caustic media that still prefers to paint Elvis *fans* as *fanatics*. The result is that new generations have become Elvis fans.

Elvis was more than just a popular performer—his long career, many shifts in image, and associations with such ideas as rebellion, sex, excess, and tragedy have rendered him an iconic or mythic figure. The Elvis legend is frequently evoked in movies, plays, and the songs of other musicians to convey an idea or make a point.

New leadership at RCA has focused on repackaging Elvis's music to emphasize its historical and musical significance. Their efforts have reinforced the idea that the true legacy of Elvis Presley is his music.

The King Is Dead

When Elvis Presley died on a hot August day in 1977, it made international headlines. From tiny Tupelo, Mississippi, to the glamorous boulevards of Paris, the world slowed down for a moment to mourn.

..."All Roads Lead to Memphis"

—London **Evening Standard**, *August 17, 1977*

"The King Is Dead"

—Tupelo **Daily Journal**, *August 17, 1977*

"A Lonely Life Ends on
Elvis Presley Boulevard"

—Memphis **Press-Scimitar**, *August 17, 1977*

"L'adieu à Elvis"

—**France-Soir**, *August 17, 1977*

"Last Stop on the Mystery Train"

—**Time**, *August 29, 1977*

"Elvis Has Left the Building"

—**Stereo Review**, *January 1978*

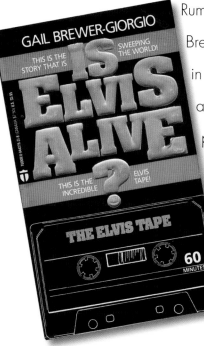

Rumors began to stir in 1979 when Gail Brewer-Giorgio wrote a novel titled *Orion*, in which the Presley-like main character arranged his own death in order to find peace and privacy. The novel generated very little attention, except that unknown singer Jimmy Ellis took the name Orion after the character in the book and then recorded several albums. He performed in public in a mask to hide his true identity, though whether he was trying to get audiences to believe he was Elvis is not known. In 1981, a book by Steven C. Chanzes claimed that a terminally ill Elvis impersonator had been interred at Graceland—not Elvis. Brewer-Giorgio's novel and Chanzes' book both flopped, and many of the rumors that had begun to surface about Elvis quickly faded.

In 1987, Brewer-Giorgio revived the rumors with her self-published book *The Most Incredible Elvis Presley Story Ever Told.* In this book, she claimed her novel *Orion* failed because it had been squelched by important Presley people. It seems the novel had gotten too close to the truth. Her claims that Elvis was still alive were based on a few unexplained mysteries in Elvis's life that she supposedly researched and then explained. Her book was republished the next year as *Is Elvis Alive?,* and her position was supported by Texas-based record producer Major Bill Smith. The resulting publicity started a full-scale media blitz, culminating in Elvis sightings in fast-food restaurants, at cheap motels, and even at Chernobyl shortly after the nuclear disaster.

"But it's hard to imagine Elvis Presley's success coming anywhere but here. He molded it out of so many American elements: country and blues and gospel and rock; a little Memphis, a little Vegas, a little arrogance, a little piety. . . . How could we ever have felt estranged from Elvis? He was a native son."

—*Charles Kuralt, CBS News Special, August 18, 1977*

BEST
Collectibles Unused Concert Tickets

Elvis was scheduled to leave on another grinding road trip on August 17, 1977. In poor physical shape, he was not looking forward to the tour, at least according to some of those around him. He had just completed a tour in June of that year, with his last performance at Market Square Arena in Indianapolis, Indiana, on June 26. Around 2:00 P.M. on August 16, Elvis Presley was found dead at Graceland. Many of the shows on the tour that never happened were already sold out. After Elvis's death, promoters offered a refund to ticket buyers. Many fans chose not to return their tickets, keeping them as souvenirs. The fans' reluctance to receive refunds caused confusion for promoters who had to account for their losses and pay cancellation fees.

Later, many fans decided to sell their tickets for several times the face value.

"Elvis Presley's death deprives our country of a part of itself. *He was unique and irreplaceable.* More than 20 years ago, he burst upon the scene with an impact that was unprecedented and will probably never be equaled. His music and his personality, fusing the styles of white country and black rhythm-and-blues, changed the face of American popular culture. His following was immense, and he was a symbol to people the world over of the vitality, rebelliousness, and good humor of his country."

—*Jimmy Carter, August 17, 1977*

Tribute Week

Each year on the anniversary of Elvis's death, thousands of fans make the pilgrimage to Memphis to commemorate the life and career of Elvis Presley. Tribute Week began unofficially the first year after Elvis's death when fans showed up in mid-August and mingled outside the music gates at Graceland. That same year, Colonel Tom Parker, with Vernon Presley in tow, held a tribute called "Always Elvis" in Las Vegas. The Colonel's event drew little interest from the fans, however, and he never organized another.

Elvis's grave site at Graceland

Currently, Tribute Week consists of seven days of activities, memorials, and gatherings. Fans visit Graceland, Humes Junior High School, Sun Studio, Beale Street, and lesser-known Presley haunts such as Lauderdale Courts and Poplar Tunes. The city welcomes the Elvis fans, who have helped turn Memphis into a thriving tourist mecca.

Other activities include Elvis trivia contests, impersonator contests, collectibles conventions, and book signings by Elvis biographers.

During tribute week, the Meditation Garden is a sea of flowers.

The emotional high point of Tribute Week is the *candlelight vigil.* This ritual has been enacted in some form or another every year since Elvis's death. On the evening of August 15, fans gather in front of the music gates at Graceland. Elvis's music is piped over a loudspeaker as people mingle and swap Elvis stories before lining up along the graffiti-covered wall. At 11:00 P.M., two or more Graceland employees walk down to the gates with a torch that has been lit from the eternal flame that marks Elvis's grave. As the gates open, the fans, each with their own lighted candle, climb silently and reverently up the hill behind the house, where they walk single file past the grave site. The procession often takes as long as six hours to pass through the Meditation Garden. It is not only a gesture of respect for Elvis, but it is proof that Elvis's fans are as faithful after his death as they were during his lifetime.

Graceland

- Elvis's mansion in Memphis was opened to the public on June 7, 1982, and soon became one of the most visited homes in America.

- Each year, approximately 650,000 visitors come through the music gates to view the sights at Graceland. The home averages more than 1,750 visitors daily and, over the course of an eight-hour day, nearly 225 visitors per hour.

- Graceland has 23 rooms, including 8 bedrooms and 4½ baths.

- When the estate decided to open Graceland, Priscilla Presley replaced the red decor in the dining room with the blue, white, and gold color scheme from the 1960s, when she lived in the mansion. The red crushed-velvet furniture, red shag carpet, and red drapes were the result of a redecoration done in 1974 by Elvis's girlfriend, Linda Thompson.

- The three televisions in the TV room were inspired by something Elvis had read about Lyndon B. Johnson, who reportedly liked to watch the news on all three networks simultaneously. Instead of the news, Elvis was likely to watch three football games or other sporting events at once.

In 1991, Graceland was placed on the National Register of Historic Places.

I'VE BEEN INSIDE GRACELAND

Top Ten Sights at Graceland

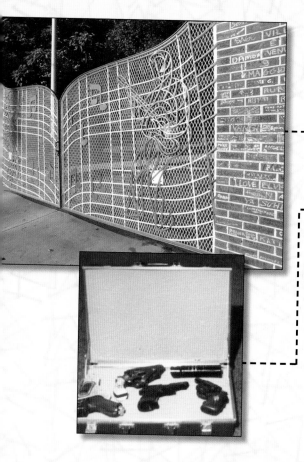

1. *Music gates*

2. Hall of Gold

3. *Firearms collection*

4. Badge collection

5. Elvis's record collection

6. RCA display of gold and platinum records

7. Meditation Garden

8. *Elvis's jet, the* Lisa Marie

9. *The pink Cadillac Elvis bought for his mother*

10. Wedding dress and suit

Shortly after Elvis died, Hollywood turned its attention to the singer once again, realizing that his enormous popularity had not been diminished by death. In 1979, ABC aired the first of several films on the life of Elvis Presley. Directed by John Carpenter, *Elvis, The Movie,* was a solid attempt to encapsulate the singer's contributions to popular music as well as to sympathetically portray Elvis the man. Kurt Russell starred as Elvis in a powerful portrayal that garnered Russell an Emmy nomination.

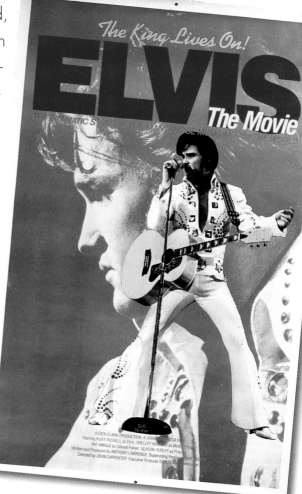

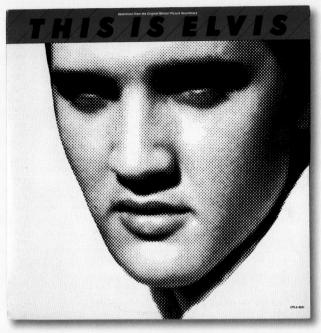

Produced, directed, and written by Andrew Solt and Malcolm Leo, *This Is Elvis* combines news footage, television performances, still photography, and re-created scenes to tell the story of Elvis's life and career. The film opens with the shocking news of the singer's death and then flashes back to his childhood years in Tupelo, Mississippi. Four different actors portray Elvis at various points in his life, including his teen years when he performs in front of his high-school class for a talent show, his mature years when he is hospitalized for numerous ailments, and on the eve of his death at Graceland. Other events and phases of his career are depicted through news footage, home movies, concert material, and still photography. Released in 1981, *This Is Elvis* was one of the first serious examinations of Elvis's life.

The King of Rock 'n' Roll:

The Complete 50's Masters

When BMG purchased RCA, they formed an international committee of record executives to clean up the Presley catalogue. Interested in presenting Elvis Presley's music as a chronicle of a culturally significant performer, the committee embarked on a multiproject goal that involved reissuing the music in as close to its original form as possible.

Released in 1992, *The King of Rock 'n' Roll: The Complete 50's Masters* represents BMG's first significant restoration effort. Producers Ernst Mikael Jorgensen and Roger Semon searched the RCA vaults from Nashville to Indianapolis to Hollywood to find what they needed for this retrospective of Elvis Presley's complete 1950s output. The purity of the sound is a result of what the producers did *not* do to the master tapes as opposed to what they did do. The five-disc, 140-track compilation fea-

tures all of Elvis's released recordings from that era as well as some alternate takes and rare live performances. A bound booklet by Presley biographer and music historian Peter Guralnik discusses the original recording sessions in depth.

Issued by the U.S. Postal Service on January 8, 1993, *the Elvis stamp* quickly became a popular and inexpensive piece of memorabilia. The stamp ballot, which featured illustrations of the two final stamp designs, has also become a desired collectible. The post office also offered a sheet of 40 stamps in a sleeve that looked like an album cover. Fans soon developed their own schemes for unique stamp collectibles, including writing erroneous addresses on Presley-stamped envelopes so they would be marked "Return to Sender."

The woman responsible for kicking off the Elvis stamp campaign was Pat Geiger. She began in 1983 with a simple letter to the U.S. Postal Service. Before she was through, more than 60,000 letters were written by stamp supporters. She wrote to celebrities seeking their support, but only Ann-Margret and her husband, Roger Smith, responded. Geiger endured endless interviews, often by an unsympathetic press, before her goal was met.

Pat Geiger died in 2005. Fans everywhere owe her a debt of gratitude for her tireless efforts.

Bill Burk and Elvis World

Elvis World is a fan newsletter that was founded in 1986 by former reporter Bill Burk. Burk's goal for *Elvis World* was to have 1,000 paid subscribers in two years. He reached that goal four days short of *EW*'s first anniversary; by November 1989, *EW* had grown to the point that Bill left his job to work on *EW* full time. When reader-

Bill with Elvis World

ship surpassed 5,000, he put a cap on subscriptions. *EW* currently reaches fans in all 50 states and 92 foreign countries. Readers have included former president Bill Clinton, the late Raisa Gorbachev, former USSR premier Boris Yeltsin, president Robert Mugabe of Zimbabwe, and Japanese prime minister Junichiro Koizumi.

Burk knew Elvis for the last 20 years of his life and wrote more than 400 newspaper articles about him. He met and became friends with many of Elvis's associates and family, which gave *EW* access to Elvis stories and photos that most other publications did not have. Burk prides himself on his accurate information and in printing rare stories and photos from people who, in many cases, have never spoken to the media before.

Bill Burk has written 13 books about Elvis and has contributed to more than 20 books written by others.

"Bill Burk has *written more good things* about my boy over the years than anyone."

—*Vernon Presley,*
August 18, 1977

From Nashville to Memphis:
The Essential 60's Masters I

This compilation of Elvis's 1960s work includes his recording sessions in Nashville and Memphis from that decade. It begins with Elvis's first sessions after his discharge from the army, which yielded the memorable album *Elvis Is Back,* and concludes with his historic sessions at American Sound Studios, which marked his successful comeback to the music scene after years of producing uninspired soundtrack albums. *The Essential 60's Masters I* leaves out the Hollywood movie soundtracks, which many consider the downfall of his musical career.

The focus on Elvis's better material from that decade allows the listener to hear the maturing of a remarkable talent. Fans of Elvis will appreciate the approach to the packaging, which offers the tracks in sequence as they were recorded. The songs in this five-disc, 130-track set were digitally remastered and include 19 previously unreleased songs. Unfortunately, Elvis's work from this decade is oblivious to the innovative rock music scene of the mid-1960s.

However, when considering that his music and films were aimed at a broad audience during that decade, the homogenous pop stylings are acceptable. Peter Guralnik authored the extensive liner notes that accompany this compilation, and his straightforward discussions of the recording sessions are detailed and insightful.

"Takin' Care of Business" was adopted by Elvis around 1970 as a slogan for himself and his organization. Many stories, embellished over time, have been handed down by the Memphis Mafia explaining why the lightning bolt was added. Some say the bolt was inspired by the insignia used by Elvis's army battalion; others claim it was simply representative of the phrase "in a flash." The most far-fetched version explains that the West Coast Mafia used a lightning bolt as a symbol, and since Elvis and his clan were dubbed the Memphis Mafia, the bolt seemed appropriate. The design for the

logo may have been worked out by Priscilla and Elvis during a plane trip, though others have claimed authorship of the logo.

Elvis on the Walk of Fame

A familiar attraction in the heart of America's movie capital, Hollywood's Walk of Fame immortalizes entertainers of the past and present. The monument consists of bronze name plaques in pink terrazzo stars embedded in the sidewalk. The stars pay tribute to the famous, the notorious, and the forgotten who made contributions to the entertainment industry. Businessperson Harry Sugarman proposed the idea

for the Walk of Fame in 1958, and announced the first eight celebrities to receive stars. Construction was completed in 1960, and the Walk of Fame was dedicated on February 9. At that time, 1,500 other performers received stars, including Elvis Presley. Currently, more than 2,000 stars make up the Walk of Fame. Each star is identified by one of five icons—a movie camera, a radio microphone, a television set, a record player, or theatrical masks. Elvis earned his star for his contributions to the recording industry.

Walk a Mile in My Shoes:
The Essential 70's Masters

This five-disc retrospective of Elvis's 1970s output features every single A- and B-side released between 1970 and August 1977. As a tribute to Elvis's concert performances, one disc features live recordings. While continuing their goal of releasing the Elvis catalogue in its original form and context, the producers also hoped to counter the negative stereotype of a garish Elvis in a white jumpsuit belting out the same Vegas-style tunes over and over.

The Essential 70's Masters dispels that image by revealing how productive Elvis was during the 1970s, despite his drug abuse and health problems. Few artists have recorded as much as Elvis did during the last six years of his life. The 120 tracks included here also indicate that Elvis was a singer with eclectic tastes, just as he was in the 1950s. He mas-

tered all manner of songs and styles and made them his own, from the baroque "An American Trilogy" to the bluesy "Merry Christmas Baby" to the country confessional "You Gave Me a Mountain." A booklet by Elvis biographer Dave Marsh offers liner notes that are informative, though his prose is more embellished than that of Peter Guralnik, who wrote the booklets for *The Complete 50's Masters* and *The Essential 60's Masters I.*

In the years since Graceland was opened to the public, countless fans have expressed their devotion to Elvis through a lively medium—*graffiti on the fieldstone wall* that borders the property. Sometimes touching, sometimes insightful, sometimes funny, these notes pay tribute to Elvis as well as comment on the many ways that he touched the lives of his fans.

"When I first heard Elvis's voice, I just knew that I wasn't going to work for anybody; and nobody was going to be my boss.... Hearing him for the first time was like busting out of jail."

—Bob Dylan, reprinted in Elvis! The Last Word, *1991*

Elvis's impersonators are probably the most curious offshoot of the collective desire to keep his name and music alive. Many people are surprised to learn that Elvis impersonators *existed long before his death. As far back as 1957, a fanzine article listing 25 important facts about Elvis Presley mentioned that he was the most impersonated entertainer in the world. In 1958, a Life magazine article remarked on the increasing number of Elvis imitators in other countries, such as Germany and Japan. Elvis was said to have enjoyed the idea that there were professional Presley impersonators.*

After Elvis died in 1977, the impersonation phenomenon blossomed into a mini-industry, and in recent years, the impersonators have become so removed from the real Elvis that they exist as entities unto themselves. Although various media have taken to ridiculing the phenomenon and, by extension, the fans

who enjoy it, no fan expects the impersonators to be as talented or as charismatic as Elvis, or even to look exactly like him. Although fans don't expect impersonators to take Elvis's place, they do enjoy them as a way to remember and relive the excitement of Elvis's live performances.

Rebel DNA

After the turn of the millennium, Lisa Marie Presley surprised the press and public by launching a music career. Her two albums reveal a hard-driving rock 'n' roll sound that is uniquely her own yet continues the tradition of her father—a fact she acknowledges in one of

her songs by declaring herself a "non-conforming s**t-starter with the rebel DNA." *To Whom It May Concern* was released in 2003, followed by *Now What* two years later.

"There have been a lotta tough guys. There have been pretenders. There have been contenders. But there is only one King."

—Bruce Springsteen

ELV1S:
30 #1 Hits

To commemorate the 25th anniversary of Elvis's death, RCA released a compilation of his number-one records titled *ELV1S: 30 #1 Hits*. The marketing campaign was designed around this tagline: "Before anyone did anything, Elvis did everything." A clever bit of phrasing, the line succinctly summarizes Elvis's contribution to pop culture history while evoking the dynamism of his sound and the danger of his original image.

The world needed to be reminded of this—and it was. *ELV1S: 30 #1 Hits* rocketed to number one when it debuted, selling 500,000 copies in its first week of release. Debuting an album in the top spot on the U.S. charts was an accomplishment Elvis had not managed while he was alive. In addition to the United States, *ELV1S: 30 #1 Hits* opened at number one in 16 other countries, including Canada, France, the United Kingdom, Argentina, and the United Arab Emirates.

Marketing strategy aside, it was the music that accounted for the CD's success. Arranged in chronological order, the compilation of hits covered Elvis's entire career at RCA—from "Heartbreak Hotel" in 1956 to "Way Down" in 1977. All the songs reached number one on the charts at the time of their original release, either in the United States or the United Kingdom. This fact softens the accusation by rock music historians who claim that Elvis's music went into severe decline during the last few years of his life. His health and career may have suffered, and his sound was no longer rock 'n' roll, but his music was still vital to large portions of his audience.

The story of Elvis's career is a universal rags-to-riches tale that still resonates with those who believe in the American Dream. Because of the symbolism inherent in his story and the global appeal of his music, Elvis has become the inspiration for many novels, plays, and musicals. In December 2009, the creative minds behind Cirque du Soleil brought to life Viva ELVIS, a combination of dance, acrobatics, and live music. Using the singer's actual voice, the show portrays Elvis as the King of Rock 'n' Roll—a musical icon who not only transformed popular music but also became a symbol of freedom, sex, and youthful rebellion.

Cast members dance during a media preview of the new Viva ELVIS show by Cirque du Soleil at the Aria hotel-casino in Las Vegas.

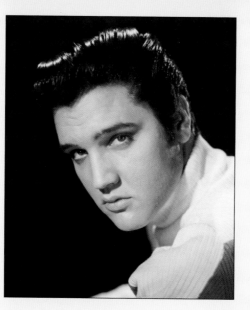

"...Elvis was and remained **a working class hero,** a man who rose from obscurity and transformed American popular art in answer to his own needs—and who may have possibly been destroyed by the isolation that being an American celebrity sometimes entails. He was as much a metaphor as a maker of music, and one of telling power and poignancy."

—John Rockwell, **The New York Times**

Index

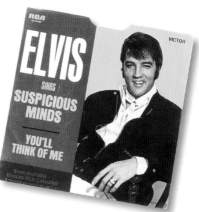

Photo credits:
Front & back cover: **PIL Collection**

AP Wide World Photos: 15, 43 (top), 44, 72, 142, 148, 219, 238; Greg Campbell, 271; Troy Glasgow, 288 (top); Mark Humphrey, 285; Stephan Savoia, 283; **Bill E. Burk Collection:** 17 (center), 18, 19, 24, 27, 53, 55, 93, 96, 109, 225, 289, 296, 297, 308; **Maria Columbus Collection:** 39, 57, 62, 65, 87, 89, 127, 141, 155, 172 (left), 229 (bottom left), 235, 247, 288 (bottom); Elvis Presley Museum, 233; Million Dollar Museum, 9; **Corbis:** 313; **Susan Doll Collection:** 85, 95; **Sharon Fox Collection:** 56, 81, 112 (bottom), 181 (top), 212, 223 (right), 242, 268 (right), 269 (top left & bottom right), 300 (top); **Getty Images:** 51, 63, 84, 91, 103, 304, 307, 314; Time Life Pictures, 88, 104, 105, 250, 279; **Globe Photos:** 305; Bob East, 97; NBC Photo, 214, 263, 265; **Heavenlea Productions:** 12, 13, 23 (top), 25, 30, 45, 149, 176, 221, 257, 258, 269 (top center & top right); **Dwight K. Irwin:** 7; **Joseph A. Krein/www.elvis2001.net:** 23 (bottom), 73, 249, 267; **Michael Ochs Archives:** Color tinting, Cheryl Winser, 37, 75, 201; **Movie Market Ltd.:** 154, 261; **Paul Lichter's Elvis Photo Archives/elvisunique.com:** 78, 79, 204 (left); **Personality Photos, Inc.:** Howard Frank, 205; **Photofest:** 33 (top), 183, 215, 241; **PIL Collection:** 5, 10–11, 17 (bottom), 21, 22, 31, 32, 33 (bottom), 41, 43 (bottom), 49, 59, 66, 67, 68, 69, 71, 76, 77, 82, 83, 99, 101, 107, 111, 112, 113, 115, 119, 129, 131, 138, 139, 143, 145, 146, 151, 156, 158, 159, 169, 170, 171, 173, 174, 175, 177, 181 (right center), 184, 187 (bottom), 189, 190, 191 (bottom), 192, 193, 196, 198, 199, 203, 206, 207 (left & right), 211, 217, 224, 227, 228, 229 (top left & top right), 230, 231, 236, 237, 243, 244, 246, 251, 253, 254, 256, 259, 262, 266, 268 (left), 269 (center & bottom left), 274, 275, 276, 280, 287 (bottom), 290, 291, 293, 299, 300 (bottom), 303, 309, 310, 311, 315, 316, 318, 319; 20th Century Fox, 121, 122, 123, 125, 163, 191 (top); Loew's Inc., 132, 133, 135, 137, 281, 317; MGM, 167, 178, 179, 188, 204 (right); MGM/United Artist Home Video, 117, 187 (bottom left & bottom right); NBC Photo, 209, 213; Paramount Pictures, 126, 166; United Artists, 163, 195; Warner Bros. Inc., 194, 197; **Retrofile:** PLP/Popperfoto, 223 (left); SAC/Popperfoto, 282; **Rockin' Robin Rosaaen~All The King's Things Collection:** 28, 29, 152, 153, 157, 161, 181 (bottom), 239, 240, 245, 264; **Showtime Archives:** Colin Escott, 20, 47, 50, 61, 74, 128, 147, 172 (right); **SuperStock:** 35, 60; © 2005 Andy Warhol Foundation for the Visual Arts, New York, 165; Karl Kummels, 255; Michael Rutherford, 295; Steve Vidler, 273, 287 (top), 301

Additional Photography: Brian Warling Studios, Dave Marsh, Sam Griffith Photography, White Eagle Studios/Dave Szarzak